CANADA
CROSSWORDS
BOOK 10

BOOK 10

DAVE MACLEOD

BARBARA OLSON

50 Themed Daily-Size Crosswords

NIGHTWOOD EDITIONS

1 2 3 4 5 6 – 13 12 11 10 09 08

Nightwood Editions
P.O. Box 1779
Gibsons, BC
V0N 1V0
www.nightwoodeditions.com

Library and Archives Canada Cataloguing in Publication

O Canada crosswords.

Bks. 1–7 written by Kathleen Hamilton. Bk. 8 written by Barbara Olson and Dave Macleod. Bks. 9–10 written by Dave Macleod and Barbara Olson.
Contents: bk. 1. 115 great Canadian crosswords — bk. 2. 50 giant weekend-size crosswords — bk. 3. 50 more giant weekend crosswords — bk. 4. 50 incredible giant weekend crosswords — bk. 5. 50 fantastic weekend crosswords — bk. 6. 50 great weekend-size crosswords — bk. 7. 50 wonderful weekend-size crosswords - bk. 8. 75 themed daily-sized crosswords — bk. 9. 75 themed daily-sized crosswords — bk. 10. 50 themed daily-sized crosswords.
ISBN 1-894404-02-5 (bk. 1).—ISBN 1-894404-04-1 (bk. 2).—
ISBN 1-894404-20-3 (bk. 5).—ISBN 0-88971-206-9 (bk. 6).—
ISBN 0-88971-218-2 (bk. 7).—ISBN 978-0-88971-217-1 (bk. 8).—
ISBN 978-0-88971-225-6 (bk. 9).—ISBN 978-088971-236-2 (bk. 10)

1. Crossword puzzles. 2. Canada—Miscellanea. I. Hamilton, Kathleen,
1942–
II. Olson, Barbara, 1963– III. Macleod, Dave, 1951–

GV1507.C7H35 2000   793.73''2   C00-910576-X

Contents

BARBARA OLSON

1 | *In the Beginning*

ACROSS

1 Slightly
5 Blow a fuse
10 Sari or Saran
14 Wee ones
15 Fred's dancing sister
16 Hot spot?
17 Long-winded one
18 * Lady aide
20 Japanese dog
22 Workplaces for *professeurs*
23 Links with
25 What Off keeps off, informally
29 * Platter choice?
31 ___-Can-Eat buffet
32 Christopher Robin's creator
35 Comm. course
36 * Signs of uncertainty?
41 "Be-Bop-A-___"
42 *Maclean's* columnist Barbara
43 Soup ingredient
46 * Canine competition
51 Top-notch person
54 Given several stars
55 Frolics about
57 Centre of Toronto?
58 * Story about Lions or Tiger-Cats, e.g.

62 Period of penitence
63 National park near Golden, BC
64 "___ directed"
65 Funny Johnson
66 Traffic sign near a park
67 Annoying ones
68 Word that can precede both parts of the answers to the starred clues

DOWN

1 Certain baseball stats
2 Part of a sequel's title
3 Comment after a failed attempt, maybe
4 African bloodsucker
5 "Gross me out!"
6 Drooling dog in *Garfield*
7 Certain Fords
8 What a "thumbs-up" signifies
9 Stop Scruffy from scratching
10 2010 Winter Olympics site
11 ___ Deer, Alberta
12 In the style of
13 Carpet layer
19 Sway drunkenly
21 Matter makeup
24 "I'll get right ___!"

26 Painter Jan van ___
27 Aussies with big pockets, for short?
28 Early riser
30 Charles Lamb's pseudonym
33 Céline Dion's name?
34 Tennyson heroine
36 "___ *dommage*" ("What a shame")
37 Humerus connection
38 Humbly admits being wrong
39 *It's ___ the Dog* (British dog-training TV show)
40 Bog buildup
41 Small business abbr.
44 The wolf ___ the door
45 Wholly enjoys
47 German prison camp
48 Not gay, briefly
49 Tooth: Comb. form
50 Classified ad word
52 Burn perfume ceremoniously
53 Fort sites
56 Kill a fly, perhaps
58 Part of DOS: Abbr.
59 One who does House work, briefly?
60 "What have we here?!"
61 Sizzling sound

Solution on page 106

2 *Thanks, Canada*

ACROSS

1 Take a sentence apart
6 Half of Québec?
10 Ferrari owner
14 Slender as ___
15 Second in a Latin lesson
16 "My treat"
17 '70s music genre
18 Murder is one
20 Typical Canadian response to "Thanks!"
22 Morales of *La Bamba*
23 "___-haw!"
24 Jeweller's measure
27 Ousted, as from office
29 Russian ruler's wife
31 Don Cherry's focus: Abbr.
32 Mrs. from Mexico
33 Not very bright
34 Typical Canadian response to "Thanks!"
40 Pop
41 Voice
42 Suspense author Levin
43 CBC Radio's *The Sunday Edition* host Michael
46 Agreed
50 Make up (for)
51 Bit of gorp
52 Tiptop
53 Typical Canadian response to "Thanks!"
57 Computer program trials
59 Family car
60 Pitcher's no-no
61 Han Solo's princess
62 Subarctic ecosystem
63 Eye annoyance
64 Tolkien baddies
65 "Does ___ any better?"

DOWN

1 Type of cell
2 Melodic
3 Fasten again
4 Arena seats are usually arranged in these
5 Ancient region bordering Palestine
6 "Out, ___ spot!" (Lady Macbeth)
7 Chew scenery
8 Husband in Hull
9 Ratio phrase
10 Leaf-related
11 Way to take things
12 Friend of François
13 Macdonald's bill
19 Ottawa pop singer Paul
21 Mascara target
25 Indigo-yielding shrub
26 Pat (down)
28 "Pipe down!"
29 Take a crack at
30 Fill beyond full
32 Austin Powers, e.g.
34 Brainstorm
35 Desire
36 In a nimble fashion
37 Carney of the Red Chamber
38 ". . . ___ quit!" (ultimatum words)
39 Got settled
44 Engine valve
45 Old tale of adventure
46 Cuban dances or sauces
47 "Get it?" (from a beatnik)
48 Make really mad
49 Observed in attendance
51 It's some kind of nerve
54 Dramatic start
55 River through Flanders
56 Italian wine-growing region
57 Kid's ammo
58 Have a bite

1	2	3	4	5	■	6	7	8	9	■	10	11	12	13
14					■	15				■	16			
17					■	18				19				
20					21								■	■
22				■	23			■	■	24			25	26
27				28			■	29	30					
■	■	■	31			■	32			■	■	33		
34	35	36				37				38	39			
40			■	■	41			■	42			■	■	■
43			44	45			■	46				47	48	49
50					■	■	51			■	52			
■	■	53			54	55				56				
57	58								■	59				
60				■	61				■	62				
63				■	64				■	65				

Solution on page 106

3 | *Pun on the Job*

ACROSS

1 Equally large
6 "Think Global, Shop ___ "
11 Point of view intro, in a chat room
14 Boggy inlet
15 As a friend, in Québec
16 Beefeater quaff
17 Interrupts, with "in"
18 Say a hundred "Hail Marys," say
20 Why the oil driller quit his job
22 Fair-hiring inits.
23 Letters to a lender
24 Shocking weapon
25 Experimentation site
27 Off one's trolley
30 ___ We Trust (US motto)
33 ". . . and to ___ good night!"
35 Casablanca's ctry.
36 Why the deep-sea diver quit his job
40 ___ *vous plaît*
41 Tire, with "out"
42 Bothersome
43 Extra: Abbr.
45 Phelps's home stretch

48 Angry clamour
50 It may be lent or bent
51 Bk. parts
54 Why the soda fountain employee quit his job
58 Watery septet
59 Award won by *Passchendaele*
60 Start to fix?
61 Response to *bitte*
62 "¿*Cómo está* ___?"
63 Frat.'s counterpart
64 Someone ___ problem
65 Does' dears

DOWN

1 American activist Hoffman
2 Cook mushrooms, say
3 Multiply ___ (double)
4 Kappa preceder
5 Wearing one's Sunday best
6 Shown to the door
7 ___ about (roughly)
8 Russian leader?
9 Accommodating
10 Several of a cod species
11 Dolt
12 Small: Pref.

13 Short race, for short
19 Left agape
21 Bruins' city: Abbr.
25 Connors with a plank
26 Finns' kin
28 Hand (over), slangily
29 Deuce topper, in cards
30 "___ deal!"
31 Reason to be barred from a bar
32 Rush reaction?
34 Produce spears
37 Gargantuan
38 Becomes raspy, as a voice
39 A 30-day mo.
44 Service station job
46 Fluffs up, at the salon
47 Ti preceders
49 *La* ___ (Montreal theme park)
51 Prefix with "-gon"
52 *Peer Gynt Suites* composer
53 Timetables, slangily
54 Recipe amts.
55 Fairy tale favourite
56 Jet Ski follower
57 *A* ___ *of God* (Margaret Laurence)

Solution on page 106

DAVE MACLEOD

4 | *Oz Query*

ACROSS

1 Scuff up
4 ___ *with Love* (1967 film)
9 Raunchy British sitcom
14 Québec's ___ d'Orléans
15 Boxer Marciano's birth name
16 Car shopper's option
17 Tavern door sign
18 Beginning of a rhetorical straw man question
20 Struck out
22 Pou ___ (vantage point, from the Greek)
23 Bookie's quote
24 It usually has twelve pockets
29 Question, part 2
34 Trip
35 When doubled, a troublesome fly
36 Newfoundland Screech, e.g.
37 On ___ (rampaging)
38 Tic
40 Juniper drink
41 AOL, for one
44 Behave as if
46 Question, part 3
49 Succulent houseplants
50 ___ the finish
53 Wear and tear
54 Montréal Canadiens, to fans
58 End of the question
63 "Bali ___"
64 Eat at
65 Kind of bore or basin
66 Russian fighter jet
67 Start of an Irish lullaby
68 Dictation whiz
69 A loooong time

DOWN

1 Marcel Marceau, e.g.
2 *Jeopardy!* host Trebek
3 Descartes or Magritte
4 Start to cycle
5 Comics punchline?
6 McGill or Dalhousie: Abbr.
7 Winter fisher's tool
8 Greenhouse problem
9 Every last drop
10 Partner of above
11 Saudi royal name
12 It's ___ state of affairs
13 Places to retire to
19 Them
21 Skin layer
25 Angel of both Islam and Christianity
26 Baseball Hall-of-Famer Hodges
27 Hoopla in Hogtown: Abbr.
28 Dietary fat substitute
29 Room at the top
30 ___ Vista
31 Hiker's route
32 One of Canada's largest energy companies
33 Noted plus-size model
34 Gives a little
39 Like thick carpeting
42 Finder of new hockey talent
43 Adjusts in advance
44 Leave speechless
45 Community facility: Abbr.
47 Like most violent films
48 Not caring anymore
50 Skeptic's comment
51 Detective Wolfe
52 Peek-___
55 Alas kin
56 Scott of sitcoms
57 Omen
59 Ball or bag contents
60 Byron wrote one to Napoleon
61 Rooter
62 Good name for a plumber?

Solution on page 106

BARBARA OLSON

5 | *Not Your Average Joe*

ACROSS

1 Flog ___ horse
6 Neck accessory clip
14 The Queen's pet pet
15 Mysterious smiler
16 Coffee-flavoured side dish with breakfast?
18 Recap, with "up"
19 Ex of "the Donald"
20 Java-loving star of *Scarface*?
27 Gull with a forked tail
28 Hole numbers at Glen Abbey
29 Battle of Britain flyers: Abbr.
33 Meeting handout
36 "___ Sides Now" (Joni Mitchell)
38 Lévesque's law
39 Popular cocktail with a caffeine kick?
42 "___ Mine" (Beatles song)
43 "... E-I-E-I-O, with ___ ..."
44 Uses a Pink Pearl
45 Legis. meeting
47 Alternative word
49 Evinrude rival, briefly
50 Jolt of java for a sleepy horse?
54 Range of influence
57 Part of TNT
58 Coffee-flavoured quaff that can be drunk like a meal?
65 Just a few
66 Played a messy Halloween trick
67 CBC Comedy Festival locale
68 Kasparov's castles

DOWN

1 Savings at BMO, e.g.
2 Vancouver band whose slogan is Talk - Action = 0
3 West ender?
4 Shocked breathless
5 Put the hook in the eye
6 Wee, in verse
7 Not pro
8 "It's ___-brainer"
9 1990s Israeli PM Yitzhak
10 Chocolate or vanilla, in the States
11 12-point type size
12 "The Heat ___" (Glenn Frey tune)
13 Greek singer Mouskouri
17 Great Big Sea song "When ___ (I can't get down)"
20 Early video game systems
21 Pod vegetable
22 Eclair fillers
23 CBC's ___ Maria Tremonti
24 CN's last car, once
25 Toothy swamp dweller, briefly
26 "Brevity ___ soul of wit": Shakespeare
30 Puts a lid on
31 Some IM users
32 Out-and-out flop
34 Strands in a laboratory
35 Topic for CBC Radio's "The Age of Persuasion"
37 Belly laugher's syllable
40 "Holy ___!"
41 Showed up
46 Show utter disdain for
48 Abbr. after a company name
51 SNL comedienne Sheri
52 Nosy one
53 Beatles beat-keeper
54 "That was ___ blow"
55 Beginning to cure?
56 Bingo call
59 Way to send docs online
60 Are outstanding?
61 Canadian comedian Abbott, for short
62 "B-I-___, B-I- ..."
63 Frightened cry
64 Ways around: Abbr.

Solution on page 107

6 *Working for CN*

ACROSS

1 Grp. for Roughriders
4 Short-order letters
7 Luke's *Star Wars* mentor
13 Old expression of disgust
14 Composer's necessity
15 "Fuggedaboudit!"
16 Grad school hurdle, often
19 Gulps down
20 Cut off
21 "Leaving on ___ Plane" (Peter, Paul and Mary)
23 Annoy, with "at"
24 CN worker's purchase after a raise, maybe?
28 Prince Valiant's son
29 American beer name
30 Bring up the rear
31 Money players
32 '60s TV kid
36 Like a new CN worker on his first day?
41 Mid-month date
42 High in calories
43 Chinese menu general
44 San Francisco area bridge and city
48 Mass transit option
49 How the CN worker cuts transportation costs?
52 ___ Friday's (restaurant chain)
53 Half of a fortnight
54 Lanchester and Martinelli
56 Places for hockey players and rock stars
58 Waits in readiness
61 Snappy comeback
62 In days past
63 That's a moray
64 Biblical songs
65 Shake hands with a one-armed bandit
66 Dir. from North Bay to Oshawa

DOWN

1 Corp. money men
2 Loud politician who stirs the masses
3 Not bothering
4 Pub pourers
5 Lenient
6 Song syllable
7 Starts
8 Pee-wee Herman trademark
9 Amin of Uganda
10 The Roadrunner's foil ___ Coyote
11 Happy as ___
12 ___-ce pas?
17 Relay race segment
18 What a CN worker does to leave town fast?
22 It's just a game, to Pierre
25 Crucifix inscription
26 Neapolitan flavour: Abbr.
27 Suffix with "cyclo-"
28 Et ___ (and others)
33 Casino supervisors
34 Keeps warmer longer, in a way
35 Bigheads
37 Man Fri.
38 Beatles' meter maid
39 ___ *saccharum* (sugar maple)
40 "Say it isn't so!"
45 Like a busy bees' nest
46 Atomic tryouts, briefly
47 Head Stooge
49 Grimm baddies
50 Michelangelo masterwork
51 Antiquated
52 Ball field cover
55 One-of-a-kind
57 Cambodia's Lon ___
59 Can opener
60 Time of your life

Solution on page 107

BARBARA OLSON

7 | *Pickup Lines*

ACROSS

1 *Man ___ Mancha*
5 Media frenzy on The Hill
10 Hindu god of death
14 Actor Peterson of *Corner Gas*
15 Admission of defeat
16 Punches without punch?
17 Cause of interest
18 Canada's Harry ___ of men's fashion
19 Rocks too much, as a boat
20 Pickup line
23 Cranky
24 Walks proudly
25 "Our Father, Who ___ Heaven, . . ."
26 Waterfront wane
29 Battle of the ___
30 Lowbrow art
32 Trans-Canada driver's no-no
34 Pickup line
40 Pit-stop additive
41 *Animal Crackers* troupe
43 Be at the head of the class?
48 TV forensic drama
50 Finito
51 River in Hull, PQ
53 Those with something on the line?
55 Pickup line
58 Encl. with a manuscript
59 Knitter's ball
60 Lo-cal
62 Verb type: Abbr.
63 Great times?: Var.
64 Hard ___ (toiling away)
65 Capone's nemesis
66 Unwelcome at the dog spa, perhaps
67 Small times?

DOWN

1 Brit. reference book
2 Composer Chopin
3 Opera script
4 Protestor's practice
5 Becomes a father
6 Dress
7 ___ Hashanah
8 Technical support caller, maybe
9 File and Edit, to an 8-Down
10 Gamer's rating
11 Farewells, to François
12 High regard
13 Be a *Canadian Idol* judge, say
21 NHL's Damphousse, for short
22 Milk vols., in the US
23 Neighbour of Afgh.
27 Pats on the back
28 Quilter's gathering
31 Dept. for medical and social issues
33 ___ Kippur
35 Catchall abbr.
36 Sham
37 Singsong sounds
38 Speed along
39 Anxious and then some
42 Yonge and Bloor: Abbr.
43 Alarm bell
44 Fuel component
45 US bomb trials
46 Stalactite and stalagmite studiers
47 Major rte.
49 Canadian poet Layton
52 Northeast Indian state
54 Bitty
56 Maker of SKÄRPT kitchen knives
57 Muhammad's ring foe, 1978
61 Little green men, in short

Solution on page 107

DAVE MACLEOD

8 | *Brrr!*

ACROSS

1 Computer screen graphic
5 Having what it takes
9 Woodwind section
14 Blue Jays complement
15 Fear of the French?
16 Sonata movement
17 Quick place to gas up
18 Lucid
19 Not infrequently
20 Like, in phrase
21 No real consolation for a frigid Canadian?
23 Island near New Guinea
25 Metric quart
26 Promote, as a cause
28 Some are made of water
33 Puts off
36 Word form for "eight"
37 Unfriendly greeting from a frigid Canadian?
42 Nutmeg spice
43 He declined the Nobel for Literature (1964)
44 Afternoon nap down south
47 Devoted attendant
51 Be a busybody
54 Done in by a knight
55 Reaction from a frigid Canadian to an off-colour joke?

60 Bounder
61 What the sky is, sometimes
62 He's good for laughs on late-night TV
63 By way of, informally
64 "It's ___ World" (James Brown)
65 Urges (with "on")
66 ___-Tass (Moscow news agency)
67 Blend, as traffic
68 Tear down in Britain
69 Being, in Old Rome

DOWN

1 Resident at the Dorchester pen
2 Viagra alternative
3 Highway entrance
4 Kind of weight or worth
5 Lhasa ___ (lapdog)
6 Listen intently
7 It's Monday in Montréal
8 Construct
9 Juliet's Act II cry
10 Big Broadway hit, slangily
11 "Hold ___ your hat!"
12 River of central Germany
13 French 101 verb
21 Showing no mercy, and then some

22 Sun, moon or eyeball
24 Enough, and more
27 Crafty
29 "Is that a fact?!"
30 Here, to Henri
31 WWII command overseas
32 Mama's boy
34 Parliamentary assent
35 Leftovers, of a sort
37 An in. has 2.54
38 Yes in Yokohama
39 Winter windshield buildup
40 And so on: Abbr.
41 It's not poetry
45 Fly with sleeping sickness
46 She's raggedy
48 Big boats in the Bedford Basin
49 Miss Canada coronets
50 Get through, as a trial
52 Pioneering Canadian physician Sir William ___ (1849–1919)
53 Alpha's opposite
55 Hoax
56 Hoarfrost
57 Canadian Khadr in Guantánamo
58 Zest
59 Score too few, in the end
63 Reason for overtime

Solution on page 107

9 Out of Order

ACROSS

1 Toronto hockey player, briefly
5 ___ the bill (pays)
10 Passed along, as email
14 Old Testament bk.
15 Stoppage of breath
16 To boot
17 Beef buy for the budget-minded?
19 Long partner
20 Show appreciation for beauty, in a way
21 Explain clearly
23 Rob of *Melrose Place*
24 Go from ___ B
25 Peke greeting
26 Prop up a birthday dessert?
31 Countrywide channel?
34 Pass, as time
35 "___ boy!"
36 *Us Weekly* rival
38 Some swordsmen's arms
40 Pasture gait
41 Tough situation
45 Ctrl+___+Del
46 Hockey equipment store wall mounts?
49 Heart-pumping action?
50 35 mm. camera: Abbr.
51 Department store founder Timothy
55 Couch surf, e.g.
58 Deep gully
59 Attendance monitor's notation
60 Camera shots on a beef-cooking show?
62 Tel ___
63 Fibber's admission
64 Unbiased: Abbr.
65 French resort city
66 Short scuffle
67 Dosage amts.

DOWN

1 Milk in Madrid
2 Returned calls, in the US
3 Doesn't have ___ to one's name
4 Ditzes
5 Prepare for a blood test, maybe
6 Turn down, with "out"
7 ___ at a time (methodically)
8 Oolong vessels
9 Sushi-bar quaff
10 Advice to one who's too drunk to drive
11 1963 role for Elizabeth Taylor
12 "I saw ___ sawing wood . . ." (tongue twister)
13 "Quit it!"
18 Chalky crayon
22 Harsh cleanser
24 Alias intro
27 Hebrew alphabet opener
28 Pronouns often separated by a slash
29 Patty Stacker brand
30 It's right on the map
31 RCMP honchos
32 "It'll ___" (soothing words)
33 Hunky-dory
37 Personal bugbear
39 "What ___!" ("Goody goody!")
42 Like a needle in a haystack
43 Volunteer's words
44 East Berlin's land, initially
47 Schubert's "The ___-King"
48 Idiot ___
52 Young 'uns: Var
53 Gain the edge
54 Egg holders
55 Custard dessert
56 Sitarist Shankar
57 Soul singer Redding
58 Take another shot
61 Luongo's domain

Solution on page 108

DAVE MACLEOD

10 *Hic*

ACROSS

1 Person with a big head
7 Dog-food name
11 Big roll of bills
14 Run through
15 Slick talker
17 Like some games at the Rogers Centre
18 Places for negligees
19 Like 101 courses: Abbr.
20 Little louse
21 Nobel Peace Prize city
22 Hardly surprising
25 Signal to get out of the way
27 In ___ (hurrying)
28 Colorado NHL team, in headlines
31 "___ bleach" (laundry advice)
32 Furtive whisper
33 Saint-___ (French Riviera resort)
35 Favourable vote
36 Made a promise at the altar
37 Forward sail
40 Comes to
41 Game with no card lower than seven
45 Actress Aimée
47 Bachman with a guitar
48 Khaki cousin
49 Skydived
51 Cake lady "Nobody doesn't like"
53 Go-___ (kid's race car)
54 Cranbrook hockey team
57 Spanish parlour
58 Fireproofing stuff
60 Underwrite
63 Gathers for later
64 Gaspé goodbyes
65 Ottawa VIP
66 Feature of this klue?
67 It's at the top of this puzzle

DOWN

1 Start to centre
2 Drink made from juniper berries
3 Greek king who had big problems with his parents
4 Writer of sardonic material
5 Drink made from barley
6 ___ Nova National Park
7 Coles Books order ID
8 Mine, to Mimi
9 Piehole
10 Lay down the lawn
11 Drink made from rye
12 Route for a 747
13 Chryslers of the '50s
16 Tweety and Sylvester, for short
22 Draft outlet
23 No. of candles on a cake, e.g.
24 Roper's rope
26 Drink made from aniseed
29 Drink made from potatoes
30 Salesperson's repertoire?
33 Observed, to Tweety Bird
34 Newspaper execs.
36 Drink made from rice
37 Goofball
38 Hurriedly
39 Drink made from corn
41 Encloses tightly
42 Active Hawaiian volcano
43 Application question, often
44 Word with up or off
46 Complete and total
48 Drink made from wine
50 Like a bimbo
52 "Take me ___, or not at all!"
55 Brilliant manoeuvre
56 Classic Bruin nickname
59 Harden, as plaster
61 Drink made from sugar cane
62 Language ending

Solution on page 108

BARBARA OLSON

11 | *It's Right Under Your Nose*

ACROSS

1 Lets up
6 Three, in Torino
9 Take a getaway, in a way
13 Fall guy
15 Down ___ (the Maritimes)
16 Dental-care choice for sensitive gums
18 David Bowie's record label
19 Explosive compounds
20 Ensnare by trickery
22 Cake maker
24 "Sound" in a Simon and Garfunkel song
25 Item in a cosmetic kit
27 Myrna who co-starred in 51-Across
28 Fourth notes
29 Subj. for some new Canadians
30 Like Adrienne Clarkson
33 Industrial sector: Abbr.
34 Wan and ill-looking
36 Not orig.
37 Be "inventive"
38 It might be on the bedpost
39 Cyclist's grip piece on some bike models
44 Strip down
45 Sprinkle with stardust, maybe
48 Freaks out
49 Roman love god
50 Father's advice?: Abbr.
51 With "*The*," 1932 film featuring a fiendish "Dr.," starring Boris Karloff
54 Hydroxyl compound
55 Comment made on arrival
56 Audiology unit
57 French possessive
58 Doozies

DOWN

1 Squiggly letters
2 In ___ (deeply unconscious)
3 American linguist William
4 Capable, slangily
5 Opt for, after much waffling
6 Horn honker
7 "Fudge!"
8 Biblical verb ending
9 Schoolmaster's rod
10 Husky-voiced Bacall
11 Fragrant perfumes
12 Morality philosopher
14 Elapsed, as time
17 Brief highs and lows
21 "Promiscuous Girl" girl
23 Jean Auel's *Earth's Children* heroine
24 Draped drapery
26 Did in
30 Do the math
31 They're first in the phone book
32 Apple variety?
33 Time pieces: Abbr.
34 Go bar-hopping
35 Bangalore babysitter
37 Calf catcher
38 Human ___ Project
40 Multi-celled structure
41 Badger at *Just For Laughs*, say
42 Monkey kin of Madagascar
43 Difficult word for Elmer Fudd
46 Indian statesman known as "Scholar"
47 Correct answers?
49 For ___ (not free)
52 UK men's magazine
53 Modern in Munich

Solution on page 108

12 Mind Your Ps and Qs

ACROSS

1 China's ___ Piao
4 Change with the times
9 Get home safely
14 250 and 604 in British Columbia
16 True blue
17 Products of some 24-Down
19 A son of Jacob and Leah
20 Go rotten
21 ___ HOOKS (carton warning)
22 Fabulous gentleman
24 Rotten
27 Confined, with "up"
28 Military fabric
29 The only Canadian Masters champ Mike
30 A-line style creator
31 Dorm denizens
32 Political favours, usually
36 There are never enough in a day
38 "The jig ___!"
39 Heartland of the Persian Empire
40 Thick-headed
42 Action on eBay
46 Hockey Hall-of-Famer Lindsay
47 Tropical fruit
48 There's a famous photo of Trudeau in one
49 Sniffle cause
50 '50s sex kitten Brigitte
51 Parliamentary faceoffs
56 Loosen, as a knot
57 Vest-like attire for John A. Macdonald
58 I.e., unabbreviated
59 Old gaiters
60 Letter after pi

DOWN

1 Eagerly receives
2 Poker player's comment
3 Federer and Nadal, for two
4 It's followed by a blessing
5 Goose plumage
6 Hurry-scurry
7 Part of KPH
8 "For shame!"
9 Noise from a soup eater
10 Loonie or toonie
11 Popeye's Olive
12 No-goodnik
13 Golf pro Ernie
15 Without ___ to one's name
18 "Je ne sais ___"
22 Just ___, skip and jump away
23 Hoop or huggy, for instance
24 Task-oriented social gatherings
25 Word after legal or hearing
26 ER honchos
28 Glove material
29 Apt rhyme for "pursue"
30 Badmouth
31 Stanley, for one
32 Kurt Browning did the first one in 1988
33 Catering dispenser
34 ___ buco (veal dish)
35 Canadien's prov.
36 Chart topper
37 Sudbury tram load
40 Surrealist painter Salvador
41 Funds
42 Like a GI series, chemically
43 Type of plant or cat
44 "Zip-A-Dee-___"
45 Starts in
47 Sacred choral work
48 Fairway vehicles
49 Gomery Inquiry spy grp.
50 Word before friend or seller
51 French "who"
52 German "and"
53 Hot time in Montréal
54 Brief rest
55 Singer Zadora

Solution on page 108

BARBARA OLSON

13 | *B Gone with You*

ACROSS

1 Forge workers
7 *Dial ___ Murder*
11 Ski-shop supply
14 "I ___ for miles and miles . . ." (The Who lyric)
15 Word before "tyme," often
16 "How was ___ know?"
17 Roller coaster that goes off the rails?
19 Hardly hard-nosed
20 Forget to set the alarm, maybe
21 It makes connections
23 Lucy's co-star
24 Scoundrel from the Emerald Isle?
28 Word for *un fédéraliste*
30 Gains an edge on
31 Carbon-based red sun, to astronomers
34 Golden ___ (senior citizen)
37 "Why don't we!"
38 Vengeful victor's cry: Var.
39 Whistle blower at the barracks?
42 That ship
43 ___ effort to . . .
45 Ants., to a lexicographer
46 Doofuses
48 Like blue movies
50 Liquid luncher
51 "A dozen croissants— PRONTO!," for example
55 *Othello* plotter
59 Roy Thomson Hall grp.
60 Utterly outrageous
62 Speed-dial letters?
64 Coven's quarters?
66 A Gershwin
67 Part of CNIB: Abbr.
68 Himalayan hiree, maybe
69 Half of a colon
70 Roy Rogers' birth name
71 Joan of Arc's crime

DOWN

1 Young Atlantic cod
2 Greyish purple
3 Mystery writer Michael
4 Russian ruler's wife
5 Fells with an axe
6 Keep from escaping, as flavour
7 "The ___ See You" (Michael Bublé)
8 Has a cow
9 Like this clue's number
10 Make over
11 Shot in the dark
12 ___ loss for words
13 Love letter letters
18 Yokel's you're
22 He's a Coward
25 Sixty minutes in Seville
26 ___ creek
27 Lisper's bane
29 Sixty minutes in Sicily
31 Eye-opening sound
32 Yemen's capital: Var.
33 "End of discussion!"
34 Band aid?
35 Rip off
36 Ill-prepared orator's sounds
40 ___ Music (Bryan Ferry band)
41 Confucian "way"
44 The pucks stop here
47 Stick in a go-cup
49 ___ one's sorrows
50 "Jiminy Cricket!"
52 In need of road repair
53 Giver's word?
54 Soothing sound
56 Love to bits
57 Sticky gels
58 The merry month ___
61 1975 Wimbledon champ
62 Little head-butter
63 In favour of
65 Suffix with "manager"

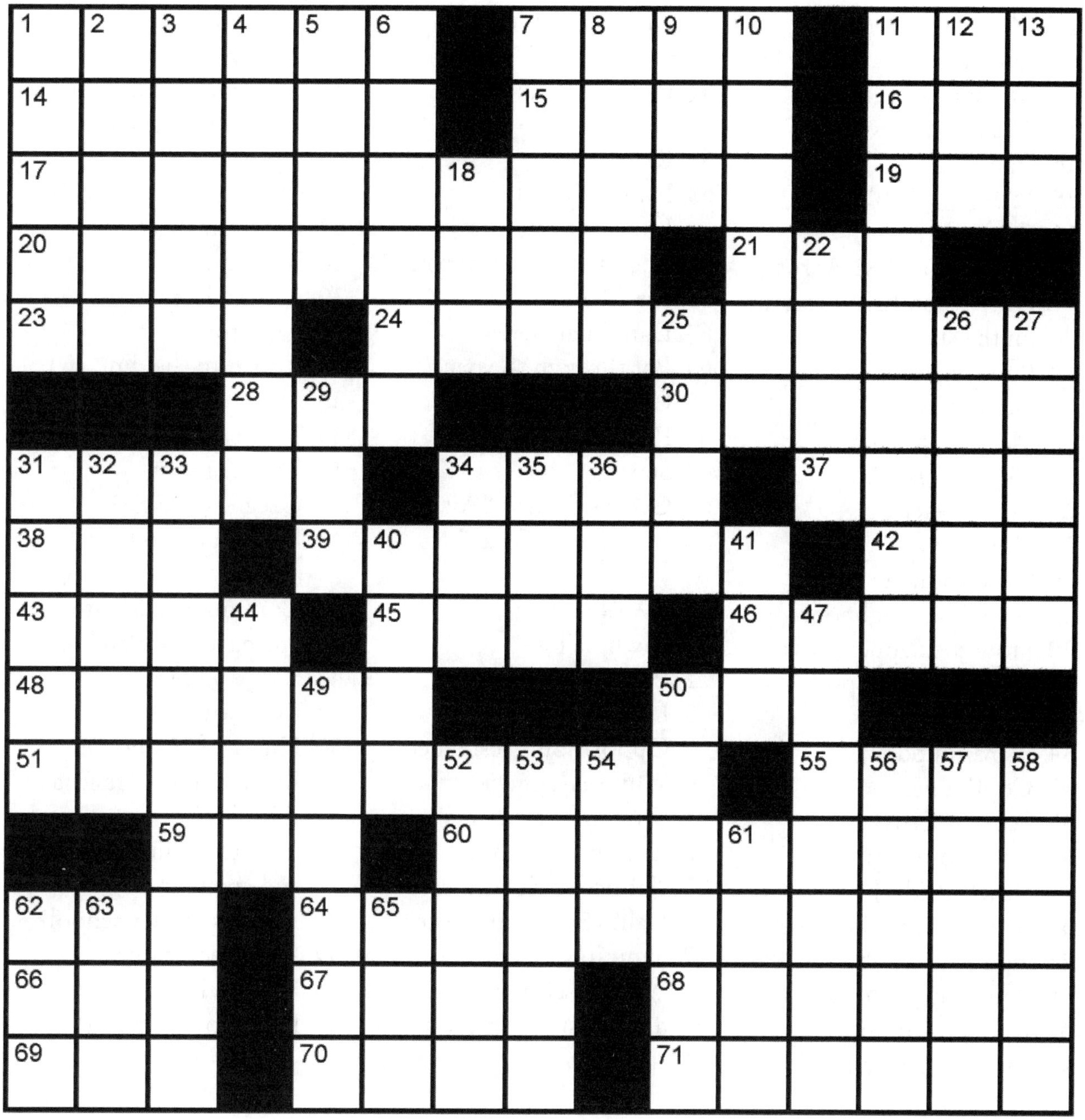

Solution on page 109

14 Money Matters

ACROSS

1 Satellite navigation letters
4 Kitchen wear
10 What you're wearing
14 Stable staple
15 "Yes ___, Bob!"
16 *Cinco y tres*
17 With 39- and 62-Across, Depression Era question on the street
19 Pop singer La ___ Jackson
20 Meryl of movies
21 City official: Abbr.
22 Torso's lack
23 Grannies
25 Shakespearean verse
27 Myanmar neighbour
29 How the dapper dress
32 ". . . even ___ speak"
33 Potent
34 Herd sound
37 Cool!, once
39 See 17-Across
40 ". . . I don't give ___." (Rhett Butler)
42 Conservative Stockwell
43 Sign of a skunk
46 Ball-shaped cheese
47 College offerings
48 Little more than

49 Famous painter of soup cans
52 Fictional Frome
54 Gag response
55 Keystone ___
58 Famed French Impressionist
61 The earth's core, mostly
62 See 17-Across
64 Dance partner?
65 Put through the paces
66 Give in to gravity
67 Place for a banjo
68 Starts
69 George Strait's "All My ___ Live in Texas"

DOWN

1 A whole lot
2 Parcel partner
3 Leader of the Opposition's residence
4 White as a ghost
5 Frisbee forerunners
6 Elementary school trio?
7 Tofino tourist draw
8 Dallas Stars star Broten
9 Submits
10 With 47-Down, modern day question on the street
11 It's often squirrelled away

12 Say wine and dine
13 Talk big
18 Cups and saucers, maybe
24 Lascivious goat-men of myth
26 Olympic legend Korbut
27 Reach the beach
28 Befuddled
30 ___-Rivières, Qué.
31 False top
34 Added to the din
35 Epps or Sharif
36 Treater's words
38 The centre of Czechoslovakia?
41 Don't take no for an answer
44 Communicates with
45 Springsteen's band name
47 See 10-Down
49 Egg beater
50 Hitter of 755 homers
51 River to Lake Geneva
53 Flip side?
56 Golf tournament for pros and amateurs
57 Avoid summer school?
59 Big screen name
60 Brief bylaws
63 Paperboy's beat: Abbr.

Solution on page 109

15 *What Did You Mean By That?*

ACROSS

1 Solo played by Harrison
4 Piles of stones serving as monuments
10 Poke in the arm
14 ___ Z (the gamut)
15 Hoofing it
16 _____ over (study)
17 "Hello."
19 Canadian attys.' degrees
20 Black's Lady
21 Funny Foxx
22 Assents at sea
23 Univ. body
25 Discharge, as sweat
27 "Hello??"
33 More liable to snap
34 *Hannah Montana* star Miley
35 Ocasek of The Cars
36 Be rude, in a way
39 Q-U connector
40 Schindler with a list
43 Disaster relief group
46 "Hell-o!!"
49 Excelled
50 Chill in the air
51 Highlands hillside
53 Brown seaweed
56 "Build it where I can't see it" acronym
60 Fast, in brand names
61 "Hel-LO-o!!"
63 Grandson of Adam
64 Rise in angry protest
65 Canada's "Sex Lady" Johanson
66 The Black Watch, for one: Abbr.
67 They have their pluses?
68 Ukr., pre-1991

DOWN

1 Outburst from Nelson on *The Simpsons*
2 *Adoration* director Egoyan (2009)
3 "Oooh, ___ get it!"
4 Radiator fluid
5 Whichever
6 "Well, ___ one am not . . ."
7 Wheel: Fr.
8 Signalled at an auction
9 Stuffy and dull
10 Glitzy and bold
11 Babysitter's nightmare
12 ". . . there ___ square"
13 Julia's role in *Ocean's Twelve*
18 Trim, as meat
24 The eight in V-8: Abbr.
26 Common list ender
27 From Limerick county, say
28 Simile meaning very ill
29 Throw in the chips
30 "___ Ben Jonson!" (literay epitaph)
31 It's Russian to the French
32 Record finishes?
33 Tweezers target
37 VCR button
38 Steinbeck's *East of ___*
41 Deity denier
42 Pi follower
44 They make you pull your own weight?
45 Adjust the corsage
47 Capital of Turkey
48 Changed direction
51 Brother, to Uncle Remus
52 '70s teen singer Simard
54 Pencil ___
55 Combustible heap
57 Tousle, as hair
58 Furnace stats
59 Belgian river
62 Third word of Canada's anthem

Solution on page 109

DAVE MACLEOD

16 | *The Named Nameless*

ACROSS

1 Once opened, they're gone
6 "___ that's your game!"
10 Where one might get a slap on the back
13 Have ___ for (adapt naturally)
14 Civic club member
16 Any one of the named nameless
18 Espresso server
19 Latin deity
20 Often
21 Fraternal gp.
23 Huff
27 What 16- and 56-Across are part of
31 Heading from Ottawa to NYC
32 Attention getters
33 Home with a flap door
34 Appalachians or Rockies: Abbr.
35 Breakfast go-with
36 Waikiki wingdings
39 Start of a gossipy remark
42 Pan Am alternative
45 What 16- and 56-Across are
48 Provoke
49 Hendrix hairdo
50 Eighth Hebrew letter
51 Longfellow's *The Bell of* ___
53 Sailor's time off
56 They're named nameless
60 Open bar feature
61 Services partner
62 Dryden of hockey and politics
63 Web addresses, for short
64 Internal conflict

DOWN

1 *Femmes* ___ (dangerous women)
2 Strong opinion start
3 Any Israeli or Arab
4 Hockey's Lindsay and Green
5 Narrow opening
6 Mork's planet
7 Cliff erosion forms these
8 *Out of Africa* star
9 Diamond Head's island
10 Paul McCartney or Elton John
11 To win the Canadian Open, you must beat it
12 In ___ event (regardless)
15 Fought like a hillbilly
17 Shaw supply
18 Vacationer's haul
22 Minuscule pollution measure: Abbr.
24 Tot's break
25 Glaciers, mostly
26 Prop at the Canadian Open
28 Dustin's *Midnight Cowboy* role
29 Sounds at 10-Across
30 Peoples' first homes
34 Plain and boring
35 Mosquito eater
36 Chowderhead
37 Cousin of Crazy Eights
38 Letters on a "Most Wanted" poster
39 Jihadist's foe
40 Referring to a ship
41 Reflected alone?
42 Steering system components
43 Rain forests, comparatively
44 Like barbecues
46 Brothers of entertainment
47 Something you might put on for show
52 Forbidden perfume?
54 Teri Garr's *Young Frankenstein* role
55 ___ one's toes (stay alert)
56 NYC airport
57 Vale Inco input
58 Kind of party
59 Some sons: Abbr.

Solution on page 109

17 *Talking Trash*

ACROSS

1 Cartoonist's chortle
5 Insect feeler
9 Sound of a 13-D
14 Port-Cartier possessive
15 "Here comes trouble"
16 Language heard in *Slumdog Millionaire*
17 Comment from a trashman, Part 1
19 Chilean "backbone"
20 They may be half or full, to a wrestler
22 Clumsy clods
23 Old TV western *The ___ Kid*
26 October gem
28 Book opener?
29 Part 2 of the comment
35 Nickname for a Nova Scotian
37 Latin "and others"
38 Wheaton of *Stand By Me*
39 Winning with no losses, early in the series
41 They're out of this world?
42 Fishing for morays
44 Low grade
46 Part 3 of the comment
48 '60s singer Sands
49 Genesis shipbuilder
50 Give a seat to

51 Typist's aids
54 "Tosca" venue
58 Shout heard during a hockey penalty
60 Conclusion to the comment
64 "You ___ Beautiful" (Joe Cocker hit)
65 Suffix with "differ"
66 Canadian-Italian Vanelli
67 Giant sound, at first?
68 In a stupor: Var.
69 They may get swollen or bruised

DOWN

1 Felon's flight
2 *Little Women* sister
3 London ___ (clothing chain)
4 Altar girl
5 Not priv.
6 Eurekas
7 Inukshuk, for the 2010 Winter Olympics
8 Disinfectant chemical
9 ___ Na Na
10 Brand at Black's
11 *Two ___ Half Men*
12 Alphabet string
13 Get lippy?
18 Old Olds
21 Skin-tight swimsuits

23 Halloween decor
24 Substitution words
25 Regatta racers
27 Play boy?
29 Solidify
30 Verb ending?
31 Moves like a flea
32 Words in a will
33 Kind of acid used in Drano
34 Blow a ___ (lose it)
36 Negative on a bilingual questionnaire
40 There's ___ in "team"
43 "Let me, really"
45 Mishmash
47 Used a lathe
50 Canadian prairie poet Mandel
51 Spanish aunts
52 Prefix with "-bat"
53 Unlikely item on a vegan menu
55 Word form for Chinese
56 Letters on a 1972 Summit Series jersey
57 Plays ___ role (is vital)
59 Get dressed
61 Stand-up's show
62 Selfish numero?
63 Batt. end

Solution on page 110

18 Reality Check

ACROSS

1 Suddenly backed off, as a horse
6 Carried on
11 West of Hollywood
14 Helsinki coin
15 Choose the window instead of the aisle?
16 Street of nightmares
17 Volunteer's offering
18 "___ me!"
19 Get ready to fire
20 Start of a statement about forgetfulness
23 Get, as a moose
24 Article in *Le Monde*
25 Lose on purpose
26 Ogopogo is one
28 Most wily
31 Occupied
32 Aladdin's vehicle
34 ___-Foy, Québec
35 More of the statement
37 Site for a cranberry crop
40 A crescendo often leads to it
41 Teapot feature
43 Grasps in all its splendour
46 Deserves
47 "The Time Machine" race
48 Pasture sound
50 ___ d'Anticosti, Gulf of Saint Lawrence
51 End of the statement
57 Hairy television cousin
58 ___ Mrs.
59 One of six simple machines
60 Roman gods
61 Stand in the corner?
62 "It's been ___ pleasure"
63 Dir. from Regina to Winnipeg
64 Like nougat
65 Piccadilly truck

DOWN

1 ___ & Span (household cleanser)
2 Overdetermined
3 Conspiring
4 Ties up, in a sense
5 Fashionable Christian
6 Champs' cry
7 Single-handedly
8 Moves away
9 *The Odyssey*, for one
10 Big name in '50s TV comedy
11 Blue ___ (*Yellow Submarine* cad)
12 Arlo's favourite restaurant
13 Kelly of clowndom
21 Cow's chew
22 Cut and paste, e.g.
26 Fleur-de-___
27 Sam of *Jurassic Park*
28 Nub
29 Mo. when DST begins
30 A group of them is a gaggle
32 Bank security devices, for short
33 Happy ___ clam
36 Kooky Caesar
37 Flood the stovetop
38 It's big on some bats
39 Sporty cars, briefly
40 Loonie, e.g.
42 First in Spain
43 Next to
44 Privileged groups
45 Bind up
46 Tattoo word
48 "Luncheon on the Grass" painter
49 In a weird way
52 Sign of things to come
53 German Mrs.
54 Hemp or jute
55 Lander at Lod
56 Every twelve mos.

Solution on page 110

BARBARA OLSON

19 *A+*

ACROSS

1 Bathtub buildup
5 Husband of Isis, in Egyptian lore
11 Home movie player
14 Water-to-wine locale
15 Fidgety feeling
16 Debtor's letters
17 Eight: Prefix
18 Scuffle
19 Ages and ages
20 Spaghetti spoon, for example?
23 Took a drive
24 Randy Bachman's boy
25 Collectible disc popular in the '90s
26 "<", mathematically
31 Watering hole for a "tea"-totaller?
35 Aerobic boxing program
36 End of Juan?
37 "___ Q" (CCR hit)
39 "Bali ___" (song from *South Pacific*)
40 Can.-US space watch grp.
43 Clothing for the smartly dressed guy?
46 Dr. Eric Foreman portrayer, on *House*
48 Classical grp. in Ontario
49 Haifa's land: Abbr.
50 Halifax Harbour haze

54 Something taken by Nunavutians for exercise?
59 Sister or mother
60 Lunchtime on graveyard shift, perhaps
61 Neet neighbour, at the drugstore
62 Spr. clock setting
63 Suavely cosmopolitan
64 They're in the mail: Abbr.
65 See 66-Across
66 Said "th" instead of 65-Across
67 Hairy Himalayan

DOWN

1 "Great ___!" ("By Jove!")
2 Place to hide gems
3 Pull some strings
4 Kettle couple of '50s flicks
5 Like a jerry-can toter, maybe
6 Up to ___ (satisfactory)
7 Happy ending, superlatively?
8 It might be on the bum?
9 Spots in the ocean
10 Overlook, as flaws
11 Competes (for)
12 Crotchety oldster
13 Words with fever or risk
21 Beginning of day, often?

22 Ian Tyson's home prov.
26 Kicks back
27 Julia's role as a legal clerk (2000)
28 Evil chuckle
29 Quatrain rhyme scheme
30 Pinot ___
31 Chinese: Comb. form.
32 Egoyan who directed *Ararat*
33 Dr. Zhivago's love
34 Speed ___
38 Highly regarded
41 Seed covering
42 Complete supply of stationery items in a writing table
44 "Pronto!"
45 Having female qualities
47 A ___ (theoretic kind of reasoning)
50 Classic Alan Ladd western
51 Ticked, and then some
52 Grass garb, in Hilo
53 Ankle-heel bones
54 They make connections
55 Unlikely hero
56 Aardvark's quarry
57 Core issues
58 Water or sand, at Glen Abbey

Solution on page 110

DAVE MACLEOD

20 *Earth Day Celebration*

ACROSS

1 ___-80, popular old RadioShack PC
4 Path left by a scythe
9 They tend to mount
14 Like a '50s cool cat
15 Supple
16 It's sometimes red
17 *Daily Gleaner* feature
19 *Opera* ___ (genre of Handel and Mozart)
20 Wish you could outdo your neighbour in recycling?
22 "That is not ___!" (parent's warning)
23 "___ goes" (Vonnegut)
24 "___ So Fine" (Chiffons hit)
25 Headed for failure
29 Beethoven's "Tempest," for one
31 ___-Dazs ice cream
34 Once, once
35 Wrong way to celebrate Earth Day?
38 Latin 101 word
40 Did Salchows
41 Get too used to
44 Colourful Southern Ontario bird
48 Calg. rival to the north

49 Show joy or sorrow
52 Zero
53 Right way to celebrate Earth Day?
58 Washer cycle
59 Help for a jalopy, often
60 More frequently, to the bard
61 Decide to join
62 Riddle-me-___ (children's book catchword)
63 Actors Mae and Adam
64 Bucks, not does
65 First First Nations NHL coach Nolan

DOWN

1 Spartan's ancient enemy
2 Head for by bus or train
3 Faucet
4 Gin flavouring
5 Prairie barricade
6 Has ___ ear (can't carry a tune)
7 Melts
8 Prefix meaning "sun"
9 Approach at a run
10 US Civil War loser Robt. ___
11 Two-time Masters winner Langer
12 Support for teapots

13 Patronizes, as a hotel
18 "Here. Have a few!"
21 "Deck the Halls" contraction
26 Feed bag tidbit
27 Church denom.
28 Self-centred concerns
30 Be cranky, as a toddler might
32 Banff wildlife sighting
33 The Arctic Circle and environs: Abbr.
35 You're wearing them
36 Actress Hagen
37 Number of ends at the Brier
38 Suffered humiliation, in a way
39 Type of crisis
42 Proprietors
43 Fire in Chicoutimi
45 Kid's racer
46 Main part of some meals
47 Took five
50 Soothing kind of bath salts
51 He's with Momma
54 "I'd hate to break up ___"
55 Part of NHL: Abbr.
56 Lake bordering Ontario
57 Neighbours of the Leafs and Habs

1	2	3	■	4	5	6	7	8	■	9	10	11	12	13
14			■	15					■	16				
17			18						■	19				
20									21					
22				■	■	■	23				■	24		
25				26	27	28	■	■	29		30			
■	■	■	31				32	33	■	■	34			
■	■	35							36	37			■	■
38	39			■	■	40					■	■	■	■
41				42	43	■	■	44				45	46	47
48			■	49		50	51	■	■	■	52			
53			54					55	56	57				
58					■	59								
60					■	61				■	62			
63					■	64				■	65			

Solution on page 110

21 *The Inn Crowd*

ACROSS

1 "There once ___ . . ." (limerick words)
5 Musical scales, e.g.
11 Sales agent
14 Airline to Haifa
15 Twin-blade razor
16 Young '___ (tots)
17 Canadian WWI flying ace
19 They're "ah"-inspiring?
20 Online loan sources
21 Article in *Der Spiegel*
22 ". . . hot in here ___ it just me?"
23 Ready to bake, as bread dough
24 *Corner Gas* writer and star
26 Stan's nickname on *Barney Miller*
28 ". . . long to ___ over us, happy and glorious . . ."
29 Mounted police, slangily
32 Kitchen addition?
34 Glass-half-empty sort
37 Something to think about
39 Homey accommodation, and this puzzle's theme
42 Emperor with a fiddle
43 Latish lunch hour
45 Nam or Cong lead-in
47 Necessity: Abbr.
48 Cul ___
51 Stirs
53 Five-time Wimbledon champ
56 Philatelist's interest
60 Pocket change for Pierre
61 ". . . girl ___ boy?"
62 University in Wolfville, NS
63 Bach's "Mass ___ Minor"
64 Longtime *As It Happens* co-host
66 Costa ___ Sol, Spain
67 Like BC's Fraser Valley
68 King of Stratford
69 Suffix meaning "jargon"
70 Flies by the seat of one's pants
71 Other than

DOWN

1 Barbecue brand
2 "I was with him," for one
3 Casa compartments
4 Just-out, in adspeak
5 Horse bettor's hangouts, briefly
6 Dernier ___ (latest fashion)
7 Subject of the Braidwood Inquiry
8 Needing more kneading, perhaps
9 Quints' name
10 Drink hot tea
11 Liquor smuggler
12 Make an ex?
13 Hissed "Hey!"
18 Informal "Catch my drift?"
22 Baby doc
24 Afghanistan's Tora ___ region
25 Half a mint?
27 Playful dig
29 Grande opening?
30 Part of 29-Across: Abbr.
31 Have blurred vision
33 ATM deposit item
35 Foul temper
36 Fancy-shmancy chicken
38 Monkey-see-monkey-doers
40 Meas. from corner to corner
41 Pepys' last word, often
44 Certain web messenger
46 Title role in a Puccini opera
49 Call with "all"
50 Pony pen
52 Well-balanced
53 Flipped LP
54 Newfoundland comedienne Cathy
55 Synagogue head
57 Challenge to ___ (fight like a knight)
58 King with a golden touch
59 Military "Father"
62 Mars's Greek counterpart
64 Ovine whine
65 Priest's robe

Solution on page 111

DAVE MACLEOD

22 | *It's Pretty Close*

ACROSS

1 Geller of spoon-bending
4 $100 notes, slangily
10 Be like a vagabond
14 Alistair who played Scrooge in 1951
15 Two-time French head Jacques
16 High hair
17 Silver-screen cowboy hero of the '40s
20 High-fashion mag
21 Banff Springs is one
22 Molson makes it
23 Greet with loud laughter
25 Any ox-eye daisy
27 Son of, in Arabic names
28 Voyageur's canoe, for one
33 Large British ref. books
34 "On the contrary, . . ."
36 Like Frankenstein's monster
38 Popular square-dance song
41 Enthusiastic bullring shout
42 Full of backtalk
45 James of spydom
48 Pop's dad: Var.
50 Mrs., in Monterrey
51 "You're in ___ of trouble!"
53 Isolate with a blizzard

55 It fell to 5% on Jan. 1, 2008
56 Fall off the rails
61 Tattletale
62 When opportunity knocks, you probably should do this
65 Algerian setting for *The Plague* by Camus
66 Noncommital response to "Will you help?"
67 Head-scratcher's comment
68 Part of NB
69 Brief arguments
70 Snake sound

DOWN

1 Celebrate the start of
2 1970 John Wayne oater
3 They enhance some silhouettes
4 XXV x X
5 Feature of *The Cat in the Hat*
6 Lodgepole, loblolly or limber
7 NHL and CFL, e.g.
8 Tex-Mex treat
9 *The Lion King* villain
10 Crimean War participant: Abbr.
11 Number for pain

12 Perplexed
13 Bill, once of *NOW* (PBS show)
18 ___ Lingus (Irish carrier)
19 CBC, for one: Abbr.
24 Bubbling
26 Empathetic statement
29 Private teacher
30 ___ Gay (1945 atom-bomb dropper)
31 They pitch stuff on TVs
32 "One-eighty" turn
35 Czech automaker
37 Edgar ___ Poe
39 Cribbage marker
40 Rises on a graph
43 Harry and William, for example
44 Blue Jay foes, sometimes
45 Spy's break-in for snooping
46 "Yeah. I bet."
47 Any guy playing tennis
49 Hitchcock classic (1960)
52 Dave Barr's org.
54 One ___ kind
57 Elevator inventor Elisha
58 "Don't look ___!"
59 Tiniest bit
60 Large battle grps.
63 Annual Vancouver fair: Abbr.
64 Golan, for instance: Abbr.

Solution on page 111

BARBARA OLSON

23 | *Down on the Farm*

ACROSS

1 Oakville vis-à-vis Toronto, briefly
5 Early 17th-century year
9 "You're soaking in it" lady
14 Miscellany
15 Fe, in chemistry
16 Alter, as legislation
17 Lorne Elliot might deliver them
19 Answers an invite
20 Reason for a mend job on the farm?
22 Fries or salad, say
23 "Just a jiffy"
27 Hog slopper of science fiction?
30 Words with shake or break
32 You'll see him in court
33 Yeats's homeland: Abbr.
34 Appointment skippers
38 West-central Canada, geographically
40 Suffix with "phys-" or "phon-"
41 *Hi and Lois* pet
43 Petro-Canada provision
44 Milkmaid who's part of a love triangle?
49 In ___ (somewhat)
50 "Horrors!"
51 Long-lasting farm implement?
57 Great devastation
60 Submarine or tank instrument
61 Pool-hall accessory
62 Util. bill
63 HS math course
64 Makes a touchdown
65 To be: Lat.
66 Splinter group

DOWN

1 Ignoramus
2 Humerus neighbour
3 Zéro
4 Spicy, as BBQ sauce
5 Mickey's girl
6 Rasta's do
7 Waist compacters?
8 Clouseau's title: Abbr.
9 Alfredo alternative
10 Dutch beer brand
11 Research partner: Abbr.
12 Canada's output stat
13 Broadbent and Stelmach
18 "May ___ who's calling?"
21 Take down a notch
24 Trail at Whistler Blackcomb
25 Spine-chilling
26 Angler's basket
27 Hertz signatory
28 Utterance of disgust
29 "You betcha"
30 Singer Bryant
31 Scot's fishing holes
35 Dryer's output?
36 Hesitant swimmer, perhaps
37 Where Bjorn was born: Abbr.
39 "___ picture paints . . ."
42 Cowers in submission
45 Develop, as a plot
46 "___ the beef?"
47 Way to serve sweet and sour
48 Many minor hockey cheerers
52 Blunted blade
53 Mos. for gobblers and goblins
54 *She ___ a Yellow Ribbon* (John Wayne movie)
55 Majestic tale
56 Princess Patricia's, for one: Abbr.
57 Stomach acid, chemically
58 "So there you are!"
59 Start to Gogh

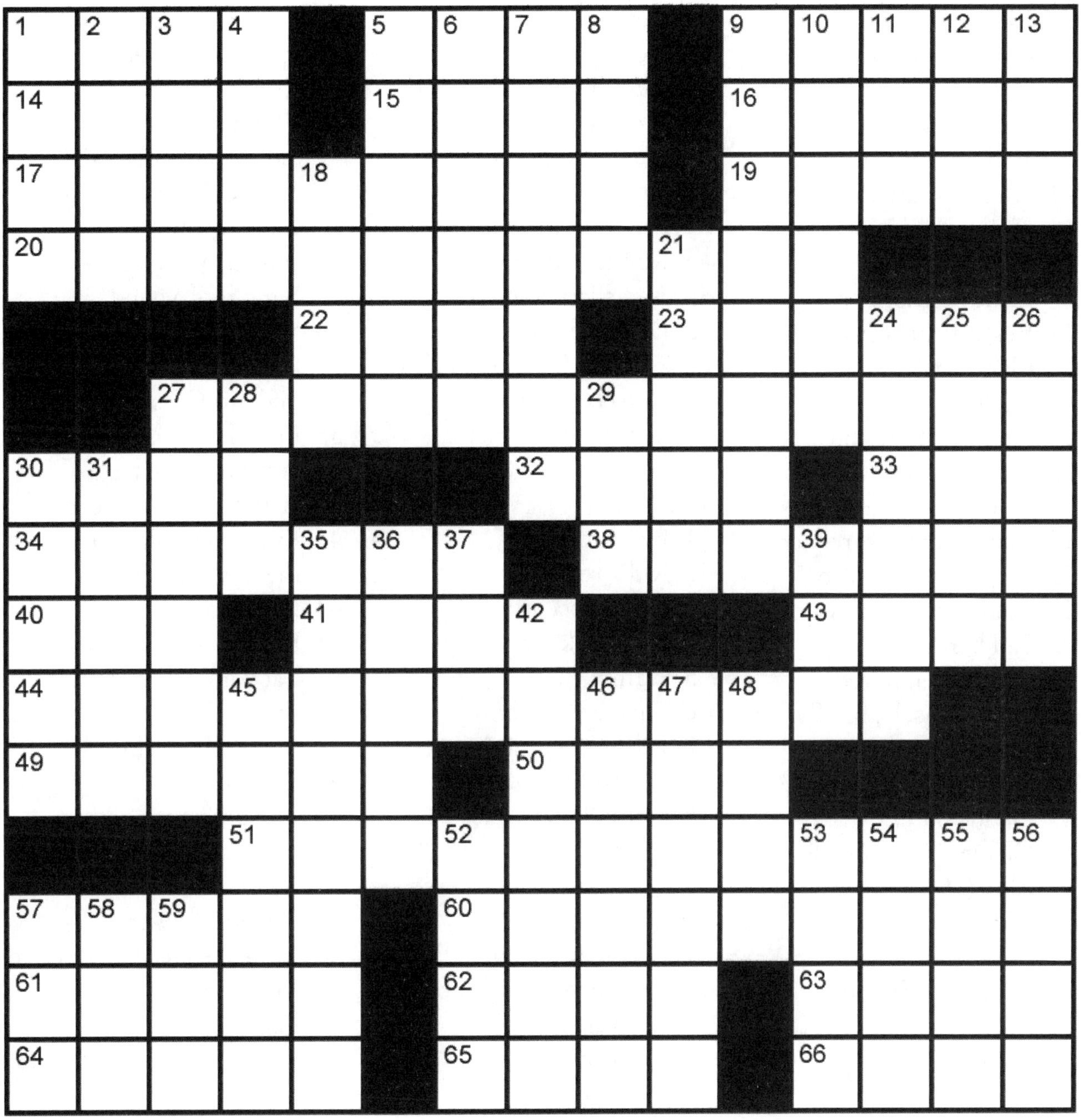

Solution on page 111

DAVE MACLEOD

24 | *At the Zoo*

ACROSS

1 Donovan Bailey excelled at this
5 Lawn headaches
10 You can't dispute it
14 ". . . ___ saw Elba"
15 Hollywood North hire
16 Hi, to Henri
17 Ernie's Muppet pal
18 Veranda on a tropical island
19 Pig food
20 Natural attraction
23 The RAF, in a famous speech by Churchill
24 They get shots frequently
25 Opposite of "paleo-"
26 French connections
27 Fall behind
30 It's written in red
32 Chest muscle, briefly
34 In ___ (petulant)
35 Rolling Stones hit (1978)
41 Divide by two
42 Chaney Jr. of *The Wolf Man* (1941)
43 "Aha!"
46 For one
48 We all pay it: Abbr.
51 Pro ___
52 Rent-___

54 Part of PQ
56 Heating or air conditioning
60 Word before over or in
61 Québec university established in 1663
62 Perfectly fitting
63 Kitchen add-on
64 At a sharp angle
65 Devil's doings
66 Zaire's Mobutu ___ Seko
67 Auto take-backs
68 Lévesque or Simard

DOWN

1 Put down
2 Kid's retort
3 Letter accents
4 Blackjack player's order
5 "Hmm . . ."
6 Final or midterm
7 Laboratory gas burners named for a volcano
8 Godzilla was one, basically
9 ___-Anne-de-Bellevue, Québec
10 Go on an extreme diet
11 Completely multipurpose
12 Converges (on)
13 Highest

21 Leather tooler's tool
22 Spanish 101 verb
28 Quick to learn
29 Thermal start
31 '60s hallucinogenic
33 Where Eskimos fend off Lions: Abbr.
35 Interest payment to the Bank of England
36 What the periodic table lists
37 Hail, to Caesar
38 French legislature
39 Smack on the head
40 Article in *Le Devoir*
41 Even good plans have them, unfortunately
44 Eye-related
45 Billy Bishop was one
47 Tachometer readout, for short
48 It's on the record
49 Exertion
50 The dot of an "i"
53 Increase the 47-Down
55 Not before
57 Chick follower
58 Roman statesman dubbed "The Censor"
59 Baja bravos

Solution on page 111

25 *Pushy Professionals*

ACROSS

1 Courses of direction
6 CD component?
10 Spr. setting in Brandon
13 ". . . ring ___ wed"
14 Emulate, as in job training
16 What an aggressive watchmaker might do
18 1990 Mohawk stand-off site
19 'Vette feature
20 Boil with anger
21 Where a Maple Leaf might fall?
23 Pi followers
25 Cries when the light goes on
26 What an aggressive lawyer might do
30 With ___ of fries
31 3-Down vessel
32 Graveyard shifts: Abbr.
33 ATM figure
36 April Fool's fool, for one
37 Banned toxic chem.
40 "Quiet!"
42 ___ fours (playing horsey)
44 What an aggressive chiropractor might do?
47 They're "borrowed" by orators
49 Computer virus search
50 Laundry cycle
51 Fly in the ointment
54 Nodder's words
56 Down East receipt fig.
57 What an aggressive cobbler might do
60 Pitch too hard, as a product
61 Comic Elliott with a big do
62 Surfer's destination, with "the"
63 Cafeteria carrier
64 Haughty look

DOWN

1 Most choosy
2 Supposed sunken island
3 Café alternative
4 *Body* ___ (William Hurt/ Kathleen Turner)
5 Post man?
6 Grad photo absentee
7 Payback promise
8 Some cameras, for short
9 Gospel singer Winans
10 Dress
11 Russian country house
12 Daycare attendees
15 Beggar's word
17 National park near Golden, BC
18 It's pedalled in church
22 Laid flat in the ring, briefly
24 Leganés ladies: Abbr.
27 High land?
28 Product safety org.
29 "Care for ___ of tea?"
34 Pen filler
35 Pen points
37 Where you can't speak freely?
38 Shut up
39 Unpointed, or to the point
40 Dolly roller
41 In an implicit way
43 Tel. book data
44 Three-legged plate
45 Brinks van cargo
46 Uses a prie-dieu
47 With ___ one's face
48 "Look ___!"
52 Skin bump, maybe
53 Groundbreaking gardener
55 Coal colour, in poesy
58 Form follower?
59 Mine find

Solution on page 112

26 *Vowel Play*

ACROSS

1 IV units
4 Dazed and confused
10 Doily fabric
14 Spa sound
15 ___ motel (tryst spot)
16 ". . . bump on ___"
17 It's on in Outremont
18 Cajoling or bootlicking
20 Get up
22 ___ the buzzer
23 Mix and purée
30 "___ silly question . . ."
31 Parliamentary focus
32 Corn serving
33 Foolish
35 Mango alternative
38 Needing very thick glasses
40 Poked provocatively
42 It's been seen before
43 Grass bristle
44 Leave ___ that
45 Bloke
49 Marilyn Monroe personified this term
54 Suffix with million or billion
55 Main artery
56 Old musket

62 ___ of Chaleur, south of the Gaspé
63 Itty bit
64 Viagra competitor
65 Is in another form
66 "___ the night before Christmas . . ."
67 In a curt and biting way
68 You'll trip on it

DOWN

1 Winter melon
2 Boorish people
3 Haunted house sound
4 Sacked out
5 Cambodia's Lon ___
6 One-time fill
7 Marshy ground
8 Songs from the sixties
9 Flash of light
10 *Chicago Hope* Emmy winner
11 Self-proclaimed "greatest"
12 Pro's opposite
13 Word with drop or roll
19 Took a load off
21 Slimy crawlers
24 Spiral-horned animal
25 South African money

26 Affirm under oath
27 Straight, as a drink
28 Not straight
29 Mexicali Mrs.
34 It's never in Germany
35 Section after A, often
36 ___ Dhabi
37 Mexican revolutionary Villa
38 U2 head
39 Clothes line
40 Chew the fat
41 Fly-by-night sort
44 Spain and Portugal together
46 Kind of tea or remedy
47 Hitching posts?
48 Fielded, as a grounder
50 Grannies
51 Accomplished
52 Pitch, in a way
53 Insolent
56 Comedian's act
57 With 59-Down, feature of limbo
58 Hagen of the stage
59 See 57-Down
60 Nth: Abbr.
61 Part of RSVP

Solution on page 112

BARBARA OLSON

27 | *The Lost Ages*

ACROSS

1 "Well, obviously!"
4 24-hour, as service
11 Wee, to Burns
14 Words before "jiffy" or "jam"
15 Ballot-box entitlement, per person
16 Mum's mum, to some
17 Daycare drop-off
18 Sneaky classroom antic
20 Fountain-pen ink, possibly?
22 Cut from *That 70's Show*
24 WNW's opposite
25 Kitchen press
26 Tickety-boo
28 Apt. rental: Abbr.
31 Course of matter?: Abbr.
32 Comment from a beaver, on completing a building project?
36 Girl's gp. on campus
37 Thus far
38 Company that's on track?
39 Hawaiian guitar whose full name means "leaping flea"
42 Getting rid of old clothing?
45 On ___ with (equal to)
48 Bus. bigwig
49 Butt ends?
50 Shakespeare's ___ *Adronicus*
52 Sylvia's partner, once

55 Tubby or Toon starter
56 Bed linen for the extra tall sleeper?
60 Lottery winner, often
61 Resistance unit
64 Letter that's silent before ess
65 Ave. crosser between Second and Fourth
66 One who stays close to home?
67 Suffix with "hex-" and "dextr-"
68 Feature of some clowns
69 Patented IDs

DOWN

1 Telegraphed tone
2 The loneliest *numero*?
3 Milliner
4 Word in a family business name
5 Winning margin at Woodbine
6 Group that represents 1.04% of Canadians
7 Tying goals
8 L-___ (Parkinson's treatment)
9 Run up ___
10 "Which is it, ___ no?"
11 Tattler
12 Martin's deputy prime minister
13 Gets someone's dander up

19 Michael of R.E.M.
21 "Yikes!"
22 Week enders: Abbr.
23 Belly laugh
27 *Divine Secrets of the ___ Sisterhood*
29 Roman 1506
30 "And ___ Love" (Kate Bush song)
33 Boat motor brand name, for short
34 The Everly Brothers' "Let ___ Me"
35 Canadian auto-parts retailer
39 Show to the door
40 Film critic Pauline
41 Choice word
42 Offering for Oliver
43 Musing by Evel Knievel?
44 Prefix meaning "bone"
45 Musical direction following *ritardando*
46 Tinkerbell and others
47 Churchill's successor
51 Nose-out-of-joint moods
53 Like cheap wine
54 Ancient Scandinavian language
57 Qatar's capital
58 Lady of Arthurian legend
59 Lab assistants?
62 "I wonder about that"
63 House party reps

1	2	3		4	5	6	7	8	9	10		11	12	13
14				15								16		
17				18							19			
		20	21											
22	23				24					25				
26				27			28	29	30		31			
32				33	34				35					
36				37				38				39	40	41
			42				43				44			
45	46	47			48					49				
50				51			52	53	54		55			
56				57	58				59					
60											61	62	63	
64				65							66			
67				68							69			

Solution on page 112

28 *Monkey Business*

ACROSS

1 Farming prefix
5 Type of food
9 ___ Walton Killam (Canadian financier)
14 Dickens' Uriah
15 Belly laugh
16 Country star Haggard
17 As a whole
19 Brought forth
20 You can't see evil
22 Memo abbr.
23 Dwarf with specs
24 They make cars and fighter jets
28 Move stealthily
33 Sporty Italian car, briefly
37 Dull as dishwater
39 Discover
40 I can't speak evil
43 Big name in handbags
44 Comic Eric
45 They stop fights, initially
46 Bad-smelling flower?
48 High-five sound
50 "Look ___ ye leap"
52 "There ___ there there" (Gertrude Stein)
56 He is unable to listen to evil
64 Kind of flu
65 Often-secret place of refuge
66 In last place, e.g.
67 The theme clues describe three wise ones in proverb
68 School type
69 Baby bouncers
70 Cries of pain
71 Middle-of-the-road

DOWN

1 Chips ___! (cookies)
2 Kind of salami
3 Debunk
4 Eye-popping paintings
5 Set-to
6 Perfect
7 Pouches
8 Staircase part
9 Doofus
10 Puzzle's centre (down south)
11 Cry of frustration
12 Ex-Expo Moisés
13 Etta of old comics
18 See-through item
21 Flapdoodle
25 Crunch targets
26 Asia's Trans ___ range
27 Leonard Cohen is one of them, to many
29 Canadian Tire spring buy, often
30 Spill the beans
31 After-lunch sandwich
32 Make-meet link
33 Array at a Bruce Cockburn event
34 Vega's constellation, with "The"
35 Scratch or dent, e.g.
36 Opera set along the Nile
38 Dante was its tour guide
41 Miss Canada, and others
42 Beaufort, for one
47 Foul up
49 Spongy branch centre
51 Long-answer question
53 West Edmonton Mall has hundreds of them
54 Surgeon's prefix
55 Caravan stops
56 Dove opposite, in politics
57 "Time ___ My Side" (Rolling Stones)
58 Royal address
59 Facility
60 Mafia chief
61 Not many
62 Capone's nemesis
63 Bank take-back, for short

Solution on page 112

BARBARA OLSON

29 Doughnuts, Anyone?

ACROSS

1 Mischievous imp
6 Toxic chem. once found in paint
9 Cha-cha cousin
14 One of Bart Simpson's aunts
15 *Ben-___*
16 Video game dinosaur?
17 High-density lipoprotein, in layman's terms
20 *The Waste Land* poet
21 Play girl?
22 Unexplored area
24 Pulling out all the stops
29 Where to see Van Dykes
31 Old British gun
32 It's found in Lac Saint-Jean
33 Overhaul, as decor
35 Shankar's strings
38 Suffix with "lact-"
39 Hockey moms' vehicles, for short
43 Reedy place
44 "Campbell's Soup Can," for one
48 Thumb-twiddling period
49 Genie summoner of fiction
52 Certain shot in the arm
57 Feature of 17-, 23- and 44-Across
59 "Zut ___!"
60 Letter recipient, sometimes
61 Slander, to a lawyer
62 CoverGirl's TruCheeks, for one
63 Fiancée's first word
64 ___ good boy deserves fudge

DOWN

1 US mil. rank
2 Corner-office occupants: Abbr.
3 Burn balm
4 DCCCL x III
5 Peace lover's principle
6 Shutterbugs
7 ___-de-sac
8 Birth coach's word
9 Doll maker
10 On the ground, to a ballerina
11 Night's end?
12 Homies in the 'hood
13 Canola and corn
18 Road rager's instrument
19 Plant offshoots
23 Its capital is Yellowknife: Abbr.
24 The "from" on a present
25 *Cat ___ Hot Tin Roof*
26 Part of a red suit
27 What tholes hold
28 Go overboard with praise
29 Crop circler
30 "___ real nowhere man . . ."
34 Earn, slangily
36 Knucklehead
37 Mai ___
40 ___-weentsy
41 Direct tel. line
42 Shows fear, in a way
45 What seekers seek, in a game
46 A bit quirky
47 Amaar of *Little Mosque on the Prairie*, e.g.
49 Melville mariner
50 Lounge on the sofa, say
51 Baseball brothers Felipe and Matty
53 CCII x II
54 "Why, ___ delighted!"
55 NY Met or LA Dodger
56 Slithery
58 Move it

Solution on page 113

30 *Picnic Fare*

ACROSS

1 Diminutive, in Dogpatch
4 The Trans-Canada is one: Abbr.
7 Show-offs, slangily
14 Strong Labatt's offering
16 Hamlet's beloved
17 Live it up
18 Throwing with effort
19 Is an expert, in other words
21 Panache
22 Sounds of sympathy
23 Sony competitor
26 Brother of Moses
31 Seemingly forever
35 Beaufort or Bering
36 Enticement
37 Is all for it
40 Bad way to be caught
41 It borders It.
42 Class struggle?
43 Is short of breath
44 One-on-one teacher
46 Jiffy
47 It comes from the heart
52 Meets expectations, in a way
58 Old northern lights
59 Anterior tooth
60 Bring down a peg
61 Feel joy or sadness about
62 Like 7-Across, covered with some of 19-, 37- and 52-Across
63 Immigrant's subj.
64 Nile nipper

DOWN

1 Beats the tar out of
2 Defeatist's words
3 "Bad, Bad ___ Brown" (Jim Croce)
4 Gets more mileage out of
5 *Entertainment Tonight* co-host, once
6 Part of a common palindrome
7 Green Giant's guffaw
8 Plays the first card
9 Bangkok native
10 "Whip It" band
11 Lena of *Chocolat*
12 Beefeater and Bombay
13 Give in to gravity
15 Play candlepins
20 Chinese restaurant condiment
24 Arthur of Wimbledon (1975)
25 Word before a maiden name
26 Drink on draft
27 Made a touchdown
28 Crass
29 Railroad carloads
30 Without ice
31 "Give it ___!" (try)
32 Actress Rowlands
33 Panache
34 Delta buildup
36 Charlie Chan's remark
38 Family girl, briefly
39 3,300-year-old king, for short
44 Giggled
45 Budding juvenile delinquent
46 City near Hamburg
48 Narc or psych ending
49 Dreadlocks wearer
50 Races in a harness
51 ___ in the bucket
52 Aide in the wings
53 Cajole
54 Rocky peaks
55 Ladies of Sp.
56 Swampy ground
57 Ones in Hull
58 Put two and two together, e.g.

Solution on page 113

31 | *The Fat Lady Sings*

ACROSS

1 ___ in the Hall ('90s comedy troupe)
5 Do goo
8 Boisterous behaviour
14 Wild way to run
15 "Who ___ to say?"
16 Infuriate
17 Actor Rob of *The West Wing*
18 Gas stove feature
20 Part of CPU
22 Folk singer DiFranco
23 Parliamentary mtg.
24 *Just For Laughs* performer
28 Fence-sitter, at times
29 Slightly short (of)
30 Pawnshop trade, mostly
34 Sound of satisfaction
35 Suffix meaning "little"
37 "Have ___ day"
38 Word with "whiz" or "willikers"
39 Nickname for Newfoundland
42 "I'm being sarcastic!"
43 Loon lookalike
45 Six letters on a phone?
46 *Carte* right?
47 X-es in, say
50 LP successors
52 Turn different colours
53 Athlete's muscle woe
56 *Born Free* feline
59 Highly interactive gaming system
60 Rain lightly
61 Pumped cleanser
65 First name in daredeviltry
67 Bun in Gretel's oven?
68 Raptors grp.
69 Do-fa filler
70 Mule-headed
71 Part of a school yr.
72 Note taker or coffee maker: Abbr.

DOWN

1 Kan opener?
2 "S'long, this ain't my scene"
3 Shabbily dressed due to poverty
4 Yarn buy
5 It may need closure
6 Brit. record label
7 Aromatic hedge bush
8 Clock the race again
9 Not in the ph. book
10 It reveals the inner you?
11 Messenger on the Hill
12 Sounds of disgust
13 Firms up
19 ___ about (roughly)
21 Argos coups
24 Bluesy Boz
25 "Fuggedaboutit!"
26 Nabors in Mayberry
27 *Out of Africa* writer Dinesen
31 Straight, hard-hit baseballs
32 Focus of *Planet Earth*
33 Parlour piece
36 Humerus's place
39 User's helpline responder
40 Grimm beginning
41 Buffalo Bill ___
44 Empty answer to "why?"
48 Gaudy, as garb
49 Madras misters
51 Finger-to-lips sounds
54 Grey Cup 2006 victors
55 Word that can follow the ends of 18-, 24-, 39-, 53- and 61-Across
56 BC border town with a giant ice cream cone
57 One with "pants on fire"
58 Small area meas.
62 Suffix with hotel
63 Homer's dad
64 Senator Wallin, to her friends
66 Feeling no pain

1	2	3	4		5	6	7		8	9	10	11	12	13
14					15				16					
17					18		19							
	20			21			22				23			
24					25	26				27				
28				29				30				31	32	33
34					35		36			37				
38				39				40	41			42		
43			44				45					46		
47					48	49		50		51		52		
			53				54				55			
56	57	58			59					60				
61				62				63	64		65			66
67						68				69				
70						71				72				

Solution on page 113

DAVE MACLEOD

32 | *A River Runs Through It*

ACROSS

1 Internet hookup device
6 ___ *Kapital* (Marx)
9 Long, loose garment
14 As a friend, to François
15 Mischievous child
16 Big name in TV infomercials
17 *Lou Grant* star
18 Coquettish
19 Of ___ (handy)
20 Put down
22 Deem necessary
23 Peter, Paul and Mary: Abbr.
24 Her gaze was "stony"
27 "Slithy" thing, to Lewis Carroll in *Jabberwocky*
28 Word in a firing sequence
29 Highest degree
30 Pivotal Algerian port in WWII
31 Start of the 18th century
33 A tiller's part of it
35 Words before glance or loss
36 Circumference
37 River that runs through Alberta into the South Sakatchewan
38 It may be blind
40 Khan who married Rita Hayworth
41 Hockey's Larionov
43 Burn with hot water
44 Spanish aunts
46 Half of nine?
47 Gave the thumbs up
48 "Don't take ___ hard"
49 Itsy-bitsy
51 Pampering place
54 Lowest points
56 Overlooked
58 Get accustomed to
59 "Welcome" rug
61 He always left his mark with a sword
62 Cruising, in a way
63 Alternatives
64 Bridge declaration
65 You, in Yucatán
66 "Takin' Care of Business" band
67 Cosmetics name

DOWN

1 Beverages for Beowulf
2 Birth
3 Quaint oaths
4 Reason for a 911 call: Abbr.
5 River that runs through New Brunswick famed for its salmon
6 Cut into cubes
7 Latin lover's word
8 Bond . . . James Bond, e.g.
9 Mötley ___
10 Get beaten by
11 Part of the Musketeers' credo
12 Got going
13 River that runs through BC to the Columbia
21 Half: Prefix
22 Canadian satirist Mort
25 Defeat in jousting
26 "Some of this, some of that" dish
28 Charade
31 They're usually armed and dangerous
32 Arid in the extreme
34 River that runs through the Territories to the Arctic Ocean
36 River that runs through Québec to the Ottawa
37 Rover's reward
39 Young fella
42 Understands
43 Care in Chicoutimi
45 Evening affair
50 Off one's rocker
51 Classic Fender guitar, for short
52 In and of itself
53 ___ of one's own medicine
55 Got between the covers?
57 Clumsy one's cry
59 Unruly bunch
60 Exhibited things

Solution on page 113

BARBARA OLSON

33 | *You're a Gem*

ACROSS

1 Green jewel
5 Blogger's "As I see it"
9 Find in an oyster bed
14 Singer Tori ___
15 Follow closely
16 By land ___
17 Given for free, slangily
18 *Hi and Lois* neighbour
19 J. Lo's last name
20 Singer Cara and others
22 *All* ___ (Martin/Tomlin comedy)
24 Inuit knife
25 Negative words
26 Blood disorder causing lethargy
28 Seed case
29 Shows disapproval, in a way
31 Arabian Peninsula native
33 Early Chinese dynasty
34 Where to see a polar bear?
37 Basic building block, and what each of the circled answers is
41 "Uh, . . . okay"
42 Jeanne ___
45 Irks
48 Roiled up
51 Scads
52 MuchMusic fare

55 It creeps around old buildings
56 Mail carrier's beat: Abbr.
57 "Must've been something ___"
58 Game of love?
60 "___ do" ("Sorry, my hands are tied")
62 Old Roman's 152
64 "Aha, now ___ it!"
65 Shake the Etch A Sketch
66 www opener
67 Heal: Lat.
68 Scorpio's stud, maybe
69 Jubilant cries
70 Australian rock?

DOWN

1 Zircon's reddish relative
2 Feeling friendly, and then some
3 Like housewives or house wines
4 Armchair athlete's channel
5 "Well, if ___ . . .!" ("Look who's here!")
6 Leave one's mark?
7 Fan's shout to the camera
8 11th-century Norse king
9 Vaulter's need
10 Spanish noun suffix

11 Comparable to "the driven snow"
12 Land a trout
13 Lapis ___
21 It's in Lac Saguenay
23 Is forbidden to, old-style
27 Makeup name
28 Modifies the Constitution
30 He might show you "the way"
32 Old MacDonald vowels
35 Places that'll leave you in stitches, for short?
36 *Grumpy Old Men* actor Davis
38 Troop grp.
39 It's new in Napoli
40 Gobbling heartily
43 Where the French fry?
44 15th anniversary gift
45 Deep red ring adornment
46 Corrida charger
47 Workboot feature
49 Cheap diner's policy
50 Enzyme ending
53 Like one with a rash reaction
54 BC's Fraser Valley city
57 Form of Agnes
59 Canadian film ____ *the Unicorn* (1998)
61 Aspirin letters
63 Amen follower?

Solution on page 114

34 | *Hollywood North*

ACROSS

1 Change from honeydew
7 Church bell sound
11 In this *localité*
14 Leaning, as letters
15 Lt. Frank Drebin, for 36-Across
16 Pet name
17 *Crash* director from Toronto (1996)
20 Go lighter
21 Caustic soda for the sink
22 Play the lotto
24 Basil-based sauce
27 Christie cookie favourite
28 Lambaste
31 Not dexterous
33 Dangerous partner
34 Path start
36 *Naked Gun* star from Regina (1988)
41 Embedded mini-map
42 Sleep problem involving breath
44 Trapeze artist
48 Refugee's goal, often
49 Former Iranian ruler
50 Less
53 "See ___ care!"
54 Is clothed in

56 Diagonal weave patterns
59 *The English Patient* author from Toronto (1996)
64 Thick ___ brick
65 Golf hazard
66 Take to one's heart
67 "___ Blu, Dipinto di Blu"
68 Cereal grains
69 Something you never should do

DOWN

1 El ___ (Spanish hero)
2 Loss leader?
3 Cut corners, maybe
4 Latin "others"
5 Auction moves
6 Go along with
7 They hold things up
8 Long stretch
9 Labatt quaff
10 Advance with interest
11 "___ Symphony" (Supremes hit)
12 Where it gets rough on the rink
13 Well situated
18 Be sorry about
19 Furrowed part of the head

22 Underwear part
23 He outranks a viscount
25 Implied
26 Skinned knee, to a kid
29 Albertville article
30 Make up on the fly
32 Soft-drink nuts
34 A sixth, in Italy?
35 Hardly any
37 ___ instant (right away)
38 Le Carré character
39 Signed up
40 Nine in Napierville
43 Montréal mate
44 Cinder fella?
45 Chicoutimi chair
46 Prankster
47 Fumbler's utterance
48 Words to the audience
51 Roofs of some 'Vettes
52 Beard on a barley seed
55 Afghanistan force: Abbr.
57 Superboy's sweetheart Lang
58 Di was one
60 Historic period
61 Delt's neighbour
62 ___ alai (game with a cesta)
63 Before, of yore

Solution on page 114

BARBARA OLSON

35 *Animal Husbandry*

ACROSS

1 Radio word before "Peter"
5 Mob groups
11 Indecisive utterances
14 Gardener's bagful
15 Without delay
16 King Cole of song
17 Check out, visually
19 "I'm c-c-cold!"
20 BC's Sea-to-___ Highway
21 "___ Thing" (much-covered song)
22 Fleury feint
23 Hike costs
27 "I can't wait!"
30 Collateral holders
31 ___ suit (baggy '40s attire)
32 Sneering distrust
35 Mourning sound
36 Ramble monotonously
37 *The Addams Family* cousin
40 Most streamlined
42 *Vingt moins neuf*
43 Not bought, as a vehicle
45 Ski bump
46 Be sure to avoid
50 Rogers and Hughes
51 It precedes a par, usually
52 Angst-ridden, informally
55 Apoc. book
56 Shift responsibility to someone else
60 Paperboy's beat: Abbr.
61 A matador might get a charge out of it
62 Stadium for Kings
63 Estonia, once: Abbr.
64 Bizet opera set in Seville
65 Angel food cake omission

DOWN

1 Gets off the fence
2 Polly's quacker?
3 Like some wine, flavour-wise
4 Summer, for Suzette
5 Wizard's work
6 Have ___ about (discuss)
7 Dinner with dipsticks?
8 Mumbai's ctry.
9 Leader of the pack
10 Rev.'s address
11 Like gumboots with a miniskirt, fashion-wise
12 Line in the sand, say
13 Verbally italicize
18 "You've Got ___" (Shania Twain)
22 Jarring sounds
23 Take (down) quickly
24 Forces on, as alcohol, with "with"
25 Embroidery loop
26 Trigger control?
27 Parts of pints: Abbr.
28 Half of a 35-Across
29 One going downhill fast?
32 Musician's buildup: Abbr.
33 Hick
34 Calgary-to-Edmonton dir.
36 Love handle?
38 Shih ___ (Tibetan dog)
39 Address book abbr.
41 Popular jeans
42 Sock-in-the-gut response
43 Some blenders
44 Atomic tryouts, briefly
45 Bit of dust
47 Soothing salt
48 Other, in Outremont
49 PM title of respect
52 Capital of Italy?
53 DCXXV x II
54 "Lay off, I get it!"
56 Chest muscle, briefly
57 Chicken ___ king
58 BC's Juan de Fuca, for one
59 Howl like a wolf

Solution on page 114

DAVE MACLEOD

36 | *Twain on Women*

ACROSS

1 Defeatist's words
6 Start of a Mark Twain quote about some women
14 Enthusiasm gone too far
15 "Not necessarily" (skeptic's comment)
16 Birch relatives
18 Gave up
19 Quote part 2
21 Geologic time period
22 Freezes over, with "up"
23 Charged atom
24 Wedding notices
26 "___ on your life!"
27 Poetic homage
28 Quote part 3
30 Cornerstone abbr.
32 Jetties
33 Quote part 4
37 Shakespearean contraction
38 Ashley Judd's mom
41 Quote part 5
43 Ticker tape, briefly?
45 ___ Lobos (Tex-Mex band)
46 Board, as a train
47 "You don't say!"
48 Canada Post datum: Abbr.
49 Back-road hazard

50 Quote part 6
53 Neighbour of the Cheyenne
56 Motor (along)
57 Americans who eat their food with relish
58 Bay window
59 End of the quote
60 Richard, the "Pocket-Rocket" of the Canadiens

DOWN

1 John Lennon hit
2 Cats with parti-coloured coats
3 Last American to win a Formula One race (1978)
4 Nobel physicist Bohr (1922)
5 Seadogs
6 "Suzanne" songwriter Leonard
7 Triumphant exclamations
8 El ___ (Pacific phenomenon)
9 Put two and two together, e.g.
10 Word on an invoice
11 Tab key function
12 Cleopatra's lover
13 Hands-up times?
17 Uttered

20 School of the future?
24 Sea north of the Aleutians
25 Between ports
27 Alec played him in *Star Wars*
28 Kind of chart
29 It's faith-based: Abbr.
31 When one might have a late lunch
32 Not "post-"
34 Ottawa VIP
35 Dull or drunk ending
36 Added, as to bread dough
39 US toy-train manufacturer Lionel, e.g.
40 From Beersheba
41 Brain-related
42 In music, a full interval higher or lower than written
43 Poet's dusk
44 Comics' Etta
46 Understand
47 Formation flyers
48 Stick out like ___ thumb
50 Kojak, to friends
51 Cornucopia, for one
52 Fireworks reaction
54 Polynesian paste
55 His father was Prince Valiant

Solution on page 114

BARBARA OLSON

37 | *Trading Places*

ACROSS

1 Wins handily
6 Book after Proverbs: Abbr.
10 Aerosols pollutants, for short
14 Sleeping sickness, of sorts
15 Husband, in Hull
16 "That was ___ blow"
17 Where ___ (the hot spot)
18 Target of Shock and Awe
19 Vane locale
20 Anne Frank's stationery needs?
23 Canada Customs arrival, perhaps
24 Holy Roman Emperor
27 Crib call
28 Lawsuit involving Conrad Black's Hollinger Inc.?
31 Frogman's tank
33 Slow: Fr.
34 Modern driver's guide, for short
37 What "everybody loves" on Canada Day, say
40 Kenmore rivals
41 Crow's foot
43 Soldier's stints
45 Ben, son of a former Prime Minister?

48 Skim alternative, briefly
52 "Only in Canada" tea
53 Quick knot tier?
55 Simile for skinny, in Iran?
58 Warhead weapon: Abbr.
60 Not worth ___
61 Gettysburg victor
62 Word with "house" or "home"
63 53-Across's destination, maybe
64 Tired travellers?
65 Razor-sharp
66 CBC listing, e.g.
67 Ejects, as lava

DOWN

1 Took by siege
2 Kia model
3 Better left ___
4 It'll make your eyes water
5 Centaur's cousin
6 Qatari honcho
7 Dear, to Domingo
8 Treetop item in a nursery rhyme
9 Drink stiffener?
10 Kicked object at an auto dealership
11 Pre-bedtime ritual, for some
12 Lovey-dovey sound

13 Personal ad abbr.
21 Invigorate
22 Knife dealer
25 ". . . believe ___ the whole thing!"
26 Québec's ___ de la Madeleine
29 US legal org.
30 Bloc Québécois, e.g.
32 Is prohibited from
34 PM Gordon Brown's domain
35 Trim (down)
36 Like most drawers
38 "You've got mail" co.
39 Bros
42 Scullers
44 Support, as a roof
46 D-flat
47 Cow that hasn't calved
49 Pain number
50 Grazing ground
51 More ___ (for the most part)
54 Priests in high places?
56 Boy in Barcelona
57 Wide-eyed
58 Tick off
59 Stick in a hall

1	2	3	4	5		6	7	8	9		10	11	12	13
14						15					16			
17						18					19			
20					21					22				
23								24					25	26
27					28	29	30							
			31	32						33				
34	35	36		37				38	39			40		
41			42				43				44			
45					46	47					48	49	50	51
52									53	54				
		55					56	57						
58	59				60					61				
62					63					64				
65					66					67				

Solution on page 115

DAVE MACLEOD

38 | *Page Layout*

ACROSS

1 China's Chairman
4 Ransacks, as drawers
10 Ocean sight from Tofino
14 Reply, in brief
15 Beastly
16 It's found in a folder
17 Lab-maze runner
18 Fell on one's face
20 Spice Girl Halliwell
22 Shih ___ (toy dogs of Lhasa)
23 Where most of Russia is
24 Copied
26 De Carlo of *The Munsters*
28 Compliment at the beach
29 Pot-belly
30 Bonehead
31 Modern forensic evidence
32 Six make a fl. oz.
33 Tattoos, for instance
37 Peel, as an apple
41 Daisy ___ of Li'l Abner
42 Cry of delight
47 Common numbers?
49 Lose effect
51 Workbook unit
52 Lake of Geneva city
53 Person who looks ahead
54 Spill the beans
55 "To ___ not to . . ."
56 One who acts with extreme caution
59 It's on in Montréal
60 In ___ (undisturbed)
61 Procrastinator's word
62 Peter Oundjian grp.
63 Sporty car roof, for short
64 Did garden work
65 The Beatles' "___ Blues"

DOWN

1 With 46-Down, qualifiers in statistics
2 Lacking iron: Var.
3 Big bird
4 Poppycock
5 "This ___ see!"
6 Paralyzed by fear
7 Israeli conservative party
8 Those, to José
9 Recital rebuke
10 Somewhat
11 Constituencies during elections
12 Win all the trophies
13 Irish airline ___ Lingus
19 Icicle's hangout
21 Tabloid twosome
25 Metaphorical small distance
26 Time for a revolution?
27 Aliens, initially
29 ___ Act (Canada's Constituton of 1867)
31 Salon supply
34 Black cat, maybe
35 ___ *Boot* (1981 U-boat movie)
36 Holiday poem opener
37 Ottawa denizen
38 Jungle movie costume
39 Meets, as a challenge
40 Backs off
43 Burnoose wearer
44 The best policy, it's said
45 Fruitless
46 See 1-Down
48 Stephen Harper is one
49 It may be classified
50 Playwright O'Neill
52 Canadian classical guitarist Boyd
54 It's found in bars
56 Winter hrs. in Prince George
57 Bands on the radio
58 "Gnarly!"

Solution on page 115

39 [sigh]

ACROSS

1 In a sad situation
7 Remembers, with "mind"
14 Equally uncommon
15 One using crib notes
16 [sigh]
18 Herbert of Pink Panther films
19 Egg on
20 Macdonald's "National Dream"
21 Tern or ern
23 Piqued, as interest
27 [sigh]
29 Sells aggressively
32 "___ my wit's end!"
33 Scot's not
34 Catch-all abbrs.
35 TO Raptors players' stats
36 ___ the pot (cause trouble)
37 Start to boil?
38 Non-stick cookware brand
40 Bobbins
42 [sigh]
45 In secrecy, briefly
46 Costs to run classifieds
50 LCD monitor's lack
51 Gets on, so to speak
52 *Scream* director Craven
53 [sigh]
57 Withdraws from an alliance
58 Breaks up with
59 Season the spuds before serving, say
60 Likes and dislikes

DOWN

1 Cries like a baby
2 ". . . moppin' a face like ___" (Murray McLauchlan lyric)
3 ___ queen (emoter)
4 Quaker bit
5 Sign in a china shop
6 Bogart toppers
7 Forwarded an email
8 "I've got it!"
9 Moon vehicle, for short
10 Blood tester's garb
11 Put a sock in it?
12 Reams out
13 Bit for Bruno
17 Antifreeze receptacles, for short
22 *A Christmas Carol* utterances
23 Sets one's sights
24 Cape Town's ctry.
25 Biz for PayPal users
26 They change colours
28 [sigh] for this puzzle, e.g.
29 ___-Bismol
30 Salt Lake City native: Var.
31 Eczema sufferer, likely
35 "Never Surrender" singer Corey
36 Sectional piece
38 Flies over Lake Victoria?
39 Help-page heading
40 Extra wager
41 Public facade, to Jung
43 "___ Toss These Oaken Ashes" (Thomas Campion)
44 Fresh body of *acqua*
47 Feature of irony
48 Word used to see who's "it"
49 Some RCMP officers
51 Deputy PM, for one
53 5 mLs
54 A neighbour of BC
55 *Frites* seasoning
56 Some GPS images

Solution on page 115

DAVE MACLEOD

 Don't Bother Me

ACROSS

1 Dry wine word
4 Scarlett of *Gone with the Wind*
9 Sign of hunger
13 Ones in Tijuana
15 Modern office manager, for short
16 Churn up
17 A Marx
18 Cheesy look?
19 Mammal with fins and teeth
20 "It's no concern of mine. Save your breath."
23 "That hurts!"
24 Drakes and bucks
25 Tory MP Ablonczy
26 "It's ___ against time!"
28 Prickly plants with purple flower heads
31 Nova Scotia beach detritus
32 Remembrance Day event
34 "It's pretty busy here. My sympathies."
40 Poker declaration
41 Per person
42 Brightens up, maybe
46 Move like a crab
47 Like a judge on the job
48 ___ Salvador

50 Prickly seed casing
51 "I have worries enough. You're on your own."
56 Prevaricates
57 Children's song refrain
58 *Return of the Jedi* green dancing girl
59 Unit of loudness
60 A hard ___ follow
61 December ditty
62 ___'acte (intermission)
63 Earthquake
64 Sot's symptoms, initially

DOWN

1 Japanese year-end party dish
2 Bewitched
3 Ontario's easternmost city
4 Davis of *Do the Right Thing*
5 Sunday songs
6 ___ *Happens* (CBC Radio 1 show)
7 Gordon Pinsent's goal
8 Rich Little, e.g.
9 Oktoberfest toast
10 From the heart (technically)
11 Creed of Christianity
12 Sylvan clearings

14 Short road warning
21 Not just any
22 '50s Ford with a push-button automatic
27 Cost-of-living stat.
28 *Un, deux,* ___
29 Triumphant cries
30 French conception
32 Pointe-Claire poppa
33 ___ all-time high
35 Buddy
36 Bud the Spud's prov.
37 Result of a fractured relationship, perhaps
38 Town that shares an airport with Tofino
39 Winter underwear
42 Atlantic salmon after one year at sea
43 Emollient
44 Playing hooky
45 Not as smart, perhaps
46 Kind of cat or cone
48 Barbecue skewers
49 "Get ___!"
52 Sri Lankan exports
53 Computer peripherals
54 Sasquatch cousin
55 When doubled, a French candy

Solution on page 115

41 | *Closet Disorganizer*

ACROSS

1 When the cock crows
7 Bones, to a doctor
11 Cheek, ironically
14 She debuted on *The Tommy Hunter Show*
15 Penn, of *Milk* (2008)
16 Journalist Medina
17 Short-sleeved separate seen on a catwalk?
19 ___ kwon do
20 Japan's largest active volcano
21 Mike Weir's concern
22 Coveted Scrabble items
24 It's the done thing?
26 Whiskered water lover
28 ___ consequence
30 Feather-filled lingerie?
33 Calgary Stampede legwear
34 Self-serving friends
35 Car coolers, for short
38 Argos' foes, at times
39 Bands on the radio
41 ___-pitch
42 *Troy* costume item
44 "Young & Restless" Canadian rockers
46 Magician's legging?
50 Campbell of *Party of Five*
51 One who pulls strings?
52 Went downhill
55 Lofty digs
57 Sch. year division
59 Cousin of Crazy Eights
60 "Well, ___ be!"
61 Upper garment for a guppy?
64 Montréal, *par exemple*
65 Suffixes with "brom-" and "chlor-"
66 Humdinger
67 Nazareth's ctry.
68 Fork-tailed gull
69 With pep in one's step

DOWN

1 Comparable to a hatter?
2 Not these
3 Set into a groove
4 *Wheel of Fortune* purchase
5 Marriage proposal word
6 Show featuring "Rex Murphy's Point of View," with "*The*"
7 ___ Kosh clothing
8 Took hold of
9 Noted existentialist
10 Start to freeze?
11 Tardy payee's penalties
12 Entangled
13 Fest in the West
18 Frame jobs
23 Meadow moans
25 Companion of 54-Down
27 Heavy wts.
29 Guesstimator's words
31 Out of ___ (misaligned)
32 Actress Rene
35 Letter header: Abbr.
36 Panaceas
37 Runny-nosed whiner: Var
39 Least fettered
40 Interprets incorrectly
43 One with a whack job?
44 Bench presser's target, for short
45 Wedding VIPs
47 Mozart's "Eine ___ Nachtmusik"
48 Sadat's predecessor
49 Hardly agile
53 Batter's place, often?
54 A Disney diminutive
56 "___ looks like a duck . . ."
58 Letter run
60 3 on the Peace Tower Clock
62 Buyer's TV channel
63 Divided Asian ctry.

Solution on page 116

42 Don't Make Me Laugh

ACROSS

1 Perhaps
6 He might be undercover
9 Set up for a fall
14 "Are you in ___?"
15 Alternative to none
16 Helpful for writing clearly, as paper
17 *SCTV* star from Toronto
19 The seven dwarfs, plus Snow White, e.g.
20 In-laws of Lennon
21 "___ Canadian!" (Molson promo)
22 How snails move
23 Jazz icon Fitzgerald
24 Some bandits have only one
25 Warty hoppers
29 Causes for repentance
31 Pronoun of Peru
35 Appalled
37 Leeriness
39 They have pressing chores
41 Afternoon treat with raisins
42 Popular bedding flower
44 Wonder of music
45 Have ___ (exert authority)
46 Barrister's bills
48 Statistician's pattern

49 ___ Tire, Canada's largest independent tire dealer
51 Not here
53 "Oh my!"
56 Cigarette ingredient
57 Hat material
61 Kind of pear
62 *Dumb and Dumber* star from Newmarket
64 Doesn't go
65 Hawaiian memento
66 It's pollution to some
67 Cloud of mosquitoes
68 Where some RNs are found
69 Keyed up

DOWN

1 Voodoo love charm
2 Cal's brother in *East of Eden*
3 Park neighbouring Banff
4 Slangy buttocks
5 "Blah, blah, blah . . .", shortly
6 Inner parts of ears
7 Kid's card game
8 Layer of wood or rubber
9 Building level
10 *This Hour Has 22 Minutes* one-time star from St. John's
11 Not in favour of, to start
12 Worm, to a salamander

13 Small whirlpool
18 Feel miserable
22 Qualifies for graduation
23 German steel city
25 Vast subarctic evergreen expanse
26 Ugly, mean tyrants
27 It's now, in Juárez
28 *Saturday Night Live* star from Ottawa
30 Oft-picked thing
32 Like James Bond, in a way
33 Welcome at the foyer
34 Noble horse
36 It's almost nothing
38 Frayed and shabby
40 Apt name for a litigant
43 More substantive
47 Relatives of gurus
50 Entertain
52 Part of a circle
53 Quick race
54 Combining form for "within"
55 Not shut, but not open either
57 Wood-cleaving tool
58 Where Blarney Castle is
59 Not more
60 West coast salmon
62 Ben Affleck's ex
63 Social worker?

Solution on page 116

BARBARA OLSON

43 | *Tangled Fishing Lines*

ACROSS

1 Nutcase
7 Spare part on a barbecue?
10 "___ you one" (grateful comment)
14 *Lingua* ___
15 Bread dispenser
16 Treats, in adspeak
17 Where some fishermen live?
19 Suffix with "symptom"
20 "Balderdash!"
21 Fifth *mois*
22 Christine of *Chicago Hope*
23 Agents who sell fishermen's catch?
27 Irking, with "off"
29 Slangy assent
30 Group spell-off
31 German-built auto
32 Genetic messenger
33 Greet the villain
34 Unemployed fisherman's classified ad?
38 Moistens
39 Grp. linked to Sinn Féin
40 She in Shawinigan
41 Ranch add-on
42 Uppermost-left key
43 Spy wear?
45 Fisherman's favourite game?
48 Beach Boys' "Fun, Fun, Fun" car
49 Part of OED: Abbr.
50 Catlike?
53 Doofus
54 What some fishermen haul their catch in?
58 Hails, in Old Rome
59 Frequently, to Frost
60 "You ___!" ("Amen!")
61 "___ Dinah" (Frankie Avalon hit)
62 Kinder Egg bonus
63 Grits' foes

DOWN

1 *Dial* ___ *Murder*
2 Pisan waterway
3 US political cartoonist Thomas ___
4 Gov't. investigation
5 Puncture opening?
6 Crocodile kin
7 ___ to go (eager)
8 Judge Lance of the Simpson case
9 Car driven by a valet, maybe
10 "Wicked Game" singer Chris
11 Where to swear
12 Special ladies?
13 Surgically removes
18 Flagston family pet
22 Cut clean
23 Compost contents
24 Rivulet
25 ___ means (not at all)
26 Understand, in CB-speak
27 Overshadow, size-wise
28 Typified
32 Letters in the den, maybe
33 ___ candle to
35 "Hey Diddle Diddle" tableware
36 *Jaws* boat
37 Charest of Québec
38 Soured, as milk
42 Air Canada ticket info.
43 CN stops
44 Most mammoth
46 Jagged-edged, as a leaf
47 Liable to snap
50 "___ only known . . ."
51 Ontario fort, lake or beach
52 Bill's added amts.
54 French word
55 Sci-fi craft
56 Southeast Asian language
57 Round fig.

Solution on page 116

DAVE MACLEOD

44 Much of Canada

ACROSS

1 Talked online
8 Too fast, likely
15 Belittle
16 With 53-Across, much of the northern Canadian forest
17 "Raise a Little Hell" band from Vancouver
18 53 minutes past
19 Tubular pasta
21 "Oy ___!"
22 With 66-Across, much of the Canadian Shield
25 Group represented by a tartan
27 Cool in the 'hood
30 It was started by Sputnik in 1957
33 Two bells in the middle watch at sea
35 "You there!"
36 Bill Haley's '50s band, with "The"
38 Big rent-a-car name
39 Much of Canada, according to Kingston's Arrogant Worms
42 Kipling mongoose Rikki-tikki-___
43 Complete
44 Herbert who played the Phantom in 1962
46 Habs Hockey Hall-of-Famer Shutt

48 Regulation at some high schools
50 Plunk or plop preceder
51 It's true in Trois-Rivières
53 See 16-Across
54 Lion sign
55 Trophy winner, for short
58 Extract used in some soft drinks
62 Against
66 See 22-Across
67 A little racier, maybe
68 Officially informed
69 Railroad bridge

DOWN

1 Summer setting in Man.
2 Part of HRH
3 In days past
4 It's of Cancer or Capricorn
5 '70s dashboard accessory
6 First place?
7 Actress Laura or her dad Bruce
8 Smarts ratings: Abbr.
9 New, as a blouse or skirt (Sp.)
10 "Yes, we ___ bananas, . . ."
11 Played ___ role
12 It's listed in the Ten Commandments
13 Nobel invention, briefly
14 Sense of self

20 Quirky
22 Library command
23 Do a surgeon's task
24 Time between flights
26 Live and ___ (1973 Bond film)
27 Go through changes
28 One of a television series
29 Stereo radio stas.
31 House of York symbol
32 Actress Plummer of Pulp Fiction
34 "No" in Edinburgh
37 Violins and violas: Abbr.
40 Not in the service: Abbr.
41 Run another taste test
42 Cluck of disapproval
45 Choice in a washroom
47 Regardless whether
49 Sir Robert L. Borden's notes, slangily
52 Way to go
54 Back street
56 Emcee
57 On ___ with
58 Cold War spy org.
59 Hockey's Bobby
60 China's Chou En-___
61 Turner of TV
63 Command to a dog
64 Slippery fish
65 Dr. of rap

Solution on page 116

45 Inflated Language

ACROSS

1 Anthem starter at a Ducks home game
5 Cranky cur's sound
8 *Citizen Kane* actor Everett
14 "This looks bad!"
15 Getty of Rush
16 Appear similar enough to represent
17 Start to an end?
19 Language of the Koran
20 How the unwanted turn up, with inflation?
22 Whitney of the cotton gin
23 Kan.'s northern neighbour
24 Hurriedly
26 Toast made in Québec
28 Lisa Simpson's instrument
30 Thrice daily, in prescriptions
31 Like this clue, numerically
33 Where iguanas are found in Canada
37 What not to take in a business deal, with inflation?
39 Eggy breakfast choice
41 Blender setting
42 In a lather, with "up"
43 Accessory for Frosty
45 ___ luxury
49 It smears in tears
53 Vowel's value in Scrabble
55 *Wheel of Fortune* buy
56 Change direction suddenly, with inflation?
59 "I Love ___" (Irving Berlin song)
60 Throaty
61 Pinhead
62 Hi-___ graphics
63 Verbal venom
64 Agreeable words: Var.
65 Bear, in Barcelona
66 Like one-star crosswords

DOWN

1 Gobs and gobs
2 Aussie gal
3 Skywalker who crossed to the dark side
4 Once-upon-a-time time
5 *The ___ and Mail*
6 Winehouse houses?
7 Rip apart
8 Tough word for Eliza Doolittle
9 Durable wood
10 Japan's "City of Water"
11 Thetford Mines industry
12 Point of carpentry?
13 Panicker's PC key
18 Average woman
21 Kiboshed
25 Masthead abbrs.
27 Inept one, slangily
29 Sleep clinic concern
32 Banned pesticide
34 Horton with a chain
35 Show friendliness, in a way
36 Prefix meaning "six"
37 Array in Stockwell Day's summer wardrobe?
38 A Coen brother, of film
39 What omega symbolizes, in physics
40 Swanson product
44 Hockey tournament handouts, often
46 Roman's "homeland"
47 Ryan and Tatum
48 First name in Canadian Arctic fiction
50 Animal stomachs
51 Singer Lennox
52 Grey areas?
54 Wacko
57 Prefix meaning "field"
58 Hick
59 ___ day now

Solution on page 117

DAVE MACLEOD

46 *Name That Beer*

ACROSS

1 Shooting irons
8 Get rid of
15 Banderas who played Zorro (2005)
16 A falling back, maybe
17 Ben-Hur's two-wheeler
18 Noisy Americans make these
19 Oldest brewer in North America (1786)
20 Michael of *Alfie* (1966)
21 Quickly, once
22 Entered the kiddie pool
23 Al Fatah's org.
26 Not pos.
27 West Edmonton Mall lineup
29 "Double, double, ___ and trouble, . . ." : *Macbeth*
30 Spy novelist John Le ___
31 Sparkled
32 Early London brewer (1840)
36 Comic movie hit of 2007
37 "In other words . . ."
38 Desert dweller
39 Parlour couches
41 Instant cash dispenser: Abbr.
44 "So's ___ old man!"
45 World Champion skater Magnussen (1973)
46 ___ pie (hon)
48 Mexican mister
49 Early London brewer (1847)
50 Do wheel work
53 Verbal counterpunch
54 Make deserving
55 Helter-___
56 It'll tickle you
57 They give finals

DOWN

1 Top video game of the 1980s
2 Like visiting health services
3 Old German prison camp
4 Bodies of art?
5 Common spice rack item
6 Royal Coat of Arms animal
7 W.C. Fields persona
8 Teen hangout
9 Misrepresents
10 Early Dartmouth brewer (1867)
11 Flimsy, as an excuse
12 TSX debut
13 Tadzhikistan, once: Abbr.
14 "___ a real nowhere man . . ." (Beatles lyric)
20 Attendant for seniors, often
22 Frayed
23 Disappearing sound
24 Queue or cue
25 Bullring bravo
28 Start to angle
29 Partner of now
30 Bay St. Lawrence, NS catch
31 Some maritime paintings
32 Apple throwaway
33 Canadian in 2006 Canada/US news
34 Mideast sultanate
35 Boy toy
36 Oldest company in North America (with "The")
39 Hang like a wind chime
40 One who deals with a pressing problem
41 One little sip, maybe
42 Tee hee
43 Some are for parking
45 Early Halifax brewer (1820)
47 Muffler clamp
48 Buttonhole, e.g.
49 Similar to
50 Official on skates, briefly
51 Dir. from Sidney to Glace Bay
52 Words before glance or loss
53 Q-U queue

Solution on page 117

BARBARA OLSON

47 Let's Get Atter!

ACROSS

1 Words with "pinch" or "pickle"
4 Alta. exemptions
8 Get ___ on (begin)
14 Hotel bed for an extra guest
15 Sound in the Strait of Georgia
16 Starfrit utensil
17 Fishing derby charge, say
19 Ump's call
20 Make a mess preparing pancakes?
22 Singer Cara and others
23 Huffy
25 Present time in Pierrefonds?
26 Kind of collision
29 MapQuest abbr.
30 Love ___ own (treat like one of us)
32 Not infrequently
34 Nonsensical talk at a certain tea party?
38 One who's had the bun
39 Great Lakes natives
40 Carpel tunnel test: Abbr.
41 Al Capone vis-à-vis income tax
44 Jolly Roger's hangout?
48 Had a giggle
50 ___-Claire, PQ
52 Noise from a busy kitchen?
55 Tear a strip off
56 Lays it on thick
57 Turn one's back on
58 Tarzan's transportation
59 Odd shoebox letters
60 Crude creatures
61 Eskimo and shepherd's
62 Québec town Val-___

DOWN

1 Strands, à la Montreal storm, 1998
2 Amateur player
3 Post-WWII Labour Party leader
4 Suffix with "neo-" or "zoo-"
5 Tap dancing sans the taps
6 Ever so dainty
7 One who looks to the future
8 What "I Love" in an Irving Berlin song
9 Tweeted on Twitter, say
10 Student stressors, often
11 Force away, as friends
12 Spring flood threat in Manitoba
13 Quattro minus uno
18 Lasted longer than expected
21 Twice daily on an Rx
24 Provincial count
27 Czech.'s continent
28 Like a lob
31 Urban exhibits
33 Slave River town, NWT
34 Computer user's first site
35 Brad's other half
36 Eur. realm until 1806
37 Movie featuring the line "Don't call me Shirley"
38 Catch the drift
42 Jag rivals
43 It's peddled by kids, often
45 Paid to play
46 Dolby ___
47 More to the point
49 Head lights?
51 Novelist Joyce Carol ___
53 Letters for "Can you make it?"
54 152 at the Forum
55 Cage component

Solution on page 117

DAVE MACLEOD

48 | *Going on a French Diet*

ACROSS

1 Flavouring for 23-Across
5 Impassive
10 Young whale
14 Scat woman Fitzgerald
15 *Gone with the Wind* family name
16 Prodigal son of Genesis
17 500 sheets of paper
18 Coup ___
19 The body's largest organ
20 Mascot of Québec's Carnaval who's on a French diet?
22 Chip or pancake amount
23 Labatt 50, e.g.
24 Belgian river to France
25 Palindromic relative
26 Don't bother
28 Perfectly acceptable
33 Town bordering Lake Simcoe
36 Small nail
37 Has intentions of
40 The Terminator and its ilk
42 Other than this
43 Spends time doing
45 Cover with ice on a large scale
47 Lawn headache
51 Time sheet total: Abbr.
52 ___ *fan tutte* (Mozart opera)
55 Randy Bachman's boy

56 Aquarium buildup
59 Town north of Montréal where everyone's on a French diet?
61 Dollar diver
62 Not at all happy with
63 The "a" of Mozart
64 Sans opposite
65 Garbo of the screen
66 Feed the hogs
67 Sahara-like
68 Presages
69 Accountant's column

DOWN

1 Kind of tea or medicine
2 Enthusiastic bullring shout
3 Jupiter, Mercury or Neptune
4 Not different
5 "Me too"
6 "___ fightin' words!"
7 Cookie type
8 "Dies ___" (Requiem Mass hymn)
9 'Dozer name
10 Popular song about being on a French diet?
11 "___ silly question, . . ."
12 Secular
13 Dejected mood
21 Some farm hands
22 Herr, here
25 Does in, as a dragon

27 Likelihood of a French diet being successful?
29 Act like a dog, sometimes
30 Sound like a dog, sometimes
31 Ugly old witch
32 Roughrider scores, for short
34 "___ a dark and stormy night . . ."
35 Ill-gotten gains
37 Actress Tilly from BC
38 Building add-on
39 Simile centre
41 David, who was Ziggy Stardust
44 Ebbed
46 Outrage
48 Habs star
49 Yogurt name
50 Doesn't suffer from insomnia
53 Speak from a soapbox, maybe
54 Misses in Mex.
56 Resigned remark
57 It's all you need, to the Beatles
58 Opera or movie suffix
59 Luau starch
60 Better than better
62 British sports car classic, in short

Solution on page 117

BARBARA OLSON

49 *The Opposite Effect*

ACROSS

1 * Yin colour, often
6 Punk rock offshoot
9 Artist noted for painting dancers
14 *Bébé*'s first word, perhaps
15 "Toots"
16 * Playpen toy
17 "___ roll!"
18 Windows XP desktop default colour
20 * St. Catharines university
22 Perrier or Evian
23 Took too much
24 Squeaks by, with "out"
26 Three, to lovers
28 Tour end?
31 Tomato-on-cement sound
33 * Building material for a pig
36 Lucy ___ Montgomery
38 Belly, briefly
39 "Yes, we can," for one
40 Tangelo type
41 * Sleight of hand
43 Eye hungrily
44 Begins, as work
46 Early second-century year
47 Pell-___ (disorderly)

48 * Split second
49 Operatic glass-shatterer
51 Big cheese eater
52 "I've ___ Strings" (*Pinocchio* song)
54 Adrienne Clarkson's husband
56 Lima's land
58 Genes' material
60 * Linguistically lacklustre
63 No matter the price
66 Trepidations
68 * Do calligraphy, say
69 Driver's one-eighty
70 Kitt and James
71 "No ___ , no feeling"
72 Some colas
73 * Yang colour, often

DOWN

1 Figure figure, for short?
2 Mary's follower
3 Cupid's other name
4 Portager's load
5 Fortes
6 Utterances from the McKenzie Brothers
7 Bit of fluff
8 Like a brief play
9 Blue Jays two-bagger: Abbr.
10 Crowded subway rider's lack

11 One who marries for money
12 Give ___ to (prompt)
13 Workplace wall hanging, briefly
19 Second smallest cont.
21 ___ oneself (was a loner)
25 Talk drunk talk
27 Sausage-shaped: Abbr.
28 "___ be going now"
29 Wiser
30 Healthy bread choice
32 Francesco's friends
34 ___ cab (prepare to leave)
35 Got down in church?
37 Liquidation World draws
39 Lake Louise winter wear
42 Smokes, briefly
45 Asian New Year
49 Wedding vow word
50 Midnight, for Cinderella
53 Official time signal grp.
55 Fib, biblically?
56 Padded feet
57 To be, in Terrebonne
59 "Hold on ___!"
61 French funnyman Jacques
62 Latin "was"
64 "___-haw!"
65 Cobb, et al.
67 Saskatoon-Regina dir.

Solution on page 118

DAVE MACLEOD

Sing Me a Song

ACROSS

1 Attacks
6 Irish Rose's lover
10 Voodoo charm
14 Good singers can carry it
15 Numbers to crunch
16 Windows rival for decades
17 Response to *bitte*
18 Rainbow shapes
19 San ___ (Italian Riviera resort)
20 He played Salieri in *Amadeus*
22 Chest beater
24 "... but for the grace of God, ___"
25 Canadian speech mannerisms
26 Poker player's challenge
29 Bridal paths
31 Philanthropist, essentially
33 Luge, for one
34 Layers of paint
35 Byrnes who played "Kookie" on *77 Sunset Strip*
36 Folksinger Gordon from Ontario
40 Song syllables
43 Udder ends
44 Confident words
48 "Oh, yeah?"
50 Smitten
52 DIY moving options

53 You might hold the mayo on this, briefly
54 Actress Long or Peeples
55 Folklore dwarf
57 It's sometimes worth a little on a lot
59 Two battalions, at least: Abbr.
61 Native of Bahrain
63 *Cinco y dos*
64 Notion in Napierville
65 Restaurant intro, often
66 Fusses
67 Raymond who played Perry Mason
68 Get loaded
69 Hägar the Horrible's dog

DOWN

1 Really enjoyed the party, in a way
2 Hot and bubbling
3 Newfoundland gets it first
4 Pop idol Paul from Ontario
5 Twitter
6 Rocker Bryan born in Ontario
7 Prevent from entering
8 Desire
9 Get comfortable with over time
10 Pop singer Anne from Nova Scotia
11 In the past

12 Carrey of comedy
13 Bouillon brand
21 Satisfied sighs
23 Playground retort
27 Down in the dumps
28 Wind down or wind up
30 The "bad" cholesterol, in letters
31 *"Je Me Souviens,"* for instance
32 Clumsy sorts
34 Princely name, in brief
37 Labignan, host of TSN's *Canadian Sportfishing*
38 Wise up
39 "Shop ___ you drop"
40 Lucy of *Kill Bill: Vol. 1* (2003)
41 Volcanic spew
42 Act drunk, in a way
45 Give in or give up
46 Cockpit denizen
47 Most proximal
49 Country star Tommy from Ontario
50 Those guys in Québec
51 Banned blasts, shortly
53 Crooner Michael from British Columbia
56 Ending with smack or switch
58 Pop star Céline from Québec
59 Make fun of
60 College website suffix
62 The Matterhorn, for one

Solution on page 118

1 ■ *In the Beginning*

```
A B I T   G O M A D   W R A P
T O T S   A D E L E   H E L L
B O R E   G I R L F R I D A Y
A K I T A   E C O L E S
T I E S T O   S K E E T E R S
S I D E O N E   A L L Y O U
    M I L N E   E C O N
  Q U E S T I O N M A R K S
L U L A   A M I E L
L E N T I L   D O G S H O W
C L A S S A C T   R A T E D A
  C A P E R S   E A T O N
S P O R T S N E W S   L E N T
Y O H O   U S E A S   A R T E
S L O W   P E S T S   G O O D
```

2 ■ *Thanks, Canada*

```
P A R S E   D E M I   F I A T
A R E E D   A M A S   O N M E
D I S C O   M O R T A L S I N
D O N T M E N T I O N I T
E S A I   Y E E   K A R A T
D E P O S E D   T S A R I N A
  N H L   S R A   D I M
I W A S H A P P Y T O H E L P
D A D   S A Y   I R A
E N R I G H T   S A I D Y E S
A T O N E   O A T   A O N E
  I T S M Y P L E A S U R E
B E T A T E S T S   S E D A N
B A L K   L E I A   T A I G A
S T Y E   O R C S   I T G E T
```

3 ■ *Pun on the Job*

```
A S B I G   L O C A L   I M O
B A Y O U   E N A M I   G I N
B U T T S   D O P E N A N C E
I T W A S B O R I N G W O R K
E E O   I O U   T A S E R
    T E S T L A B   D A F T
I N G O D   A L L A   M O R
T O O M U C H P R E S S U R E
S I L   P O O P   P E S K Y
A D D L   L A S T L A P
  F U R O R   E A R   P G S
T H E B O S S W A S A J E R K
S E V E N S E A S   G E N I E
P R E   D A N K E   U S T E D
S O R   E L S E S   S T A G S
```

4 ■ *Oz Query*

```
M A R   T O S I R   A B F A B
I L E   R O C C O   L E A S E
M E N   I F H E O N L Y H A D
E X E D   S T O   O D D S
    E G G C A R T O N
A B R A I N W O U L D T H E
S T U M B L E   T S E   R U M
A T E A R   S P A S M
G I N   I S P   A C T L I K E
S C A R E C R O W T R U L Y
  A L O E V E R A S
I N A T   U S E   H A B S
B E B E T T E R O F F   H A I
E R O D E   T I D A L   M I G
T O O R A   S T E N O   E O N
```

5 ■ Not Your Average Joe

```
A D E A D . S C A R F P I N
C O R G I . M O N A L I S A
C A N A D I A N O B A C O N
. . . S U M . . I V A N A .
A L C A P P U C C I N O . .
T E R N . . P A R S . R C A F
A G E N D A . B O T H . L O I
R U M A N D M O C H A C O L A
I M E . A M O O . E R A S E S
S E S S . E L S E . . M E R C
. . . P O N Y E S P R E S S O
A M B I T . . . T R I . . .
L A T T E F O R D I N N E R .
O N E O R T W O . . E G G E D
W I N N I P E G . R O O K S
```

6 ■ Working for CN

```
C F L . B L T . . O B I W A N
F I E . E A R . . N O D I C E
O R A L E X A M . S W I L L S
S E V E R . . A J E T . E A T
. B I G T I C K E T I T E M .
A R N . A N H E U S E R . . .
L A G . P R O S . . . O P I E
I N B A S I C T R A I N I N G
I D E S . . . R I C H . T S O
. . S A N M A T E O . B U S
O P T S T O C A R P O O L .
T G I . W E E K . . E L S A S
A R E N A S . S T A N D S T O
R E T O R T . . A G O . E E L
P S A L M S . . B E T . S S E
```

7 ■ Pickup Lines

```
O F L A . S C R U M . M A R A
E R I C . I L O S E . A D E S
D E B T . R O S E N . T I P S
. D R I V E T H R U Q U E U E
P E E V I S H . . S T R U T S
A R T I N . E B B . S E X E S
K I T S C H . U E Y . . . .
. C O M E H E R E O F T E N .
. . . S T P . M A R X E S .
T E A C H . C S I . K A P U T
O T T A W A . . R E E L E R S
C H E V Y S I L V E R A D O .
S A S E . S K E I N . L I T E
I N T R . A E O N S . A T I T
N E S S . M A N G Y . S E C S
```

8 ■ Brrr!

```
I C O N . A B L E . O B O E S
N I N E . P E U R . R O N D O
M A R T . S A N E . O F T E N
A L A . C O L D C O M F O R T
T I M O R . L I T R E . . .
E S P O U S E . . B O D I E S
. . D E L A Y S . . O C T O
C H I L L Y R E C E P T I O N
M A C E . . S A R T R E . .
S I E S T A . A C O L Y T E
. . . S N O O P . S L A I N
F R O Z E N S M I L E . C A D
L I M I T . L E N O . T H R U
A M A N S . E G G S . I T A R
M E R G E . R A S E . E S S E
```

9 ■ *Out of Order*

10 ■ **Hic**

11 ■ *It's Right Under Your Nose*

12 ■ *Mind Your Ps and Qs*

13 ■ B Gone with You

S	M	I	T	H	S	█	M	F	O	R	█	W	A	X
C	A	N	S	E	E	█	O	L	D	E	█	I	T	O
R	U	N	A	W	A	Y	R	I	D	E	█	L	A	X
O	V	E	R	S	L	E	E	P	█	A	N	D	█	█
D	E	S	I	█	I	R	I	S	H	R	O	G	U	E
█	█	█	N	O	N	█	█	O	N	E	U	P	S	█
C	S	T	A	R	█	A	G	E	R	█	L	E	T	S
H	A	H	█	A	R	M	Y	R	A	T	█	S	H	E
I	N	A	N	█	O	P	P	S	█	A	S	S	E	S
R	A	T	E	D	X	█	█	S	O	T	█	█	█	█
P	A	S	T	R	Y	R	U	S	H	█	I	A	G	O
█	█	T	S	O	█	U	N	H	E	A	R	D	O	F
K	P	H	█	W	I	T	C	H	E	S	R	O	O	M
I	R	A	█	N	A	T	L	█	S	H	E	R	P	A
D	O	T	█	S	L	Y	E	█	H	E	R	E	S	Y

14 ■ Money Matters

G	P	S	█	A	P	R	O	N	S	█	G	A	R	B
O	A	T	█	S	I	R	R	E	E	█	O	C	H	O
B	R	O	T	H	E	R	C	A	N	█	T	O	Y	A
S	T	R	E	E	P	█	A	L	D	█	A	R	M	S
█	█	N	A	N	A	S	█	█	S	O	N	N	E	T
L	A	O	S	█	N	A	T	T	I	L	Y	█	█	█
A	S	W	E	█	S	T	R	O	N	G	█	M	O	O
N	E	A	T	O	█	Y	O	U	█	A	D	A	M	N
D	A	Y	█	S	T	R	I	P	E	█	E	D	A	M
█	█	█	C	L	A	S	S	E	S	█	M	E	R	E
W	A	R	H	O	L	█	E	T	H	A	N	█	█	█
H	A	H	A	█	K	O	P	█	R	E	N	O	I	R
I	R	O	N	█	S	P	A	R	E	A	D	I	M	E
S	O	N	G	█	T	E	S	T	E	D	█	S	A	G
K	N	E	E	█	O	N	S	E	T	S	█	E	X	S

15 ■ What Did You Mean By That?

H	A	N	█	C	A	I	R	N	S	█	S	H	O	T
A	T	O	█	O	N	F	O	O	T	█	P	O	R	E
H	O	W	D	O	Y	O	U	D	O	█	L	L	B	S
A	M	I	E	L	█	R	E	D	D	█	A	Y	E	S
█	█	█	F	A	C	█	E	G	E	S	T	█	█	█
I	S	A	N	Y	B	O	D	Y	T	H	E	R	E	█
B	R	I	T	T	L	E	R	█	C	Y	R	U	S	█
R	I	C	█	S	T	A	R	E	█	R	S	T	█	█
O	S	K	A	R	█	R	E	D	C	R	O	S	S	█
W	H	A	T	H	A	V	E	W	E	H	E	R	E	█
█	S	H	O	N	E	█	N	I	P	█	█	█	█	█
B	R	A	E	█	K	E	L	P	█	N	I	M	B	Y
R	E	D	I	█	A	R	E	Y	O	U	N	U	T	S
E	N	O	S	█	R	E	A	R	U	P	█	S	U	E
R	E	G	T	█	A	D	D	E	R	S	█	S	S	R

16 ■ The Named Nameless

█	F	I	S	T	S	█	O	H	S	O	█	S	P	A
█	A	F	E	E	L	█	R	O	T	A	R	I	A	N
█	T	O	M	D	I	C	K	O	R	H	A	R	R	Y
B	A	R	I	S	T	A	█	D	E	U	S	█	█	█
A	L	O	T	█	B	P	O	E	█	S	N	I	T	█
G	E	N	E	R	A	L	P	O	P	U	L	A	C	E
S	S	E	█	A	H	E	M	S	█	T	E	P	E	E
█	█	M	T	S	█	█	B	E	D	█	█	█	█	█
L	U	A	U	S	█	I	H	E	A	R	█	T	W	A
U	N	K	N	O	W	N	E	N	T	I	T	I	E	S
G	O	A	D	█	A	F	R	O	█	H	E	T	H	█
█	█	A	T	R	I	█	L	I	B	E	R	T	Y	█
J	O	H	N	A	N	D	J	A	N	E	D	O	E	█
F	R	E	E	B	E	E	R	█	G	O	O	D	S	█
K	E	N	█	U	R	L	S	█	A	N	G	S	T	█

17 ■ Talking Trash

18 ■ Reality Check

19 ■ A+

20 ■ Earth Day Celebration

21 ■ *The Inn Crowd*

22 ■ *It's Pretty Close*

23 ■ *Down on the Farm*

24 ■ *At the Zoo*

25 ■ Pushy Professionals

```
P A T H S ■ D I S C ■ C D T
I T H E E ■ R O L E P L A Y
C L E A N Y O U R C L O C K
O K A ■ T T O P ■ S E E T H E
R I N K ■ R H O S ■ A H A S
G E T O N Y O U R C A S E ■ ■
A S I D E ■ T A S S E ■ ■ ■
N T S ■ P I N ■ S A P ■ P C B
■ ■ C A N I T ■ O N A L L
■ T A L K B A C K T O Y O U
E A R S ■ S C A N ■ S P I N
G L I T C H ■ I S E E ■ H S T
G I V E Y O U T H E B O O T
O V E R S E L L ■ L O R N E
N E T ■ T R A Y ■ S N E E R
```

26 ■ Vowel Play

```
C C S ■ I N A F O G ■ L A C E
A H H ■ N O T E L L ■ A L O G
S U R ■ B L A N D I S H I N G
A R I S E ■ ■ I N A T ■ ■ ■
B L E N D E R S E T T I N G S
A S K A ■ L A W S ■ ■ E A R
■ ■ I N A N E ■ P A P A Y A
■ B L I N D A S A B A T ■
G O O S E D ■ R E R U N ■ ■
A W N ■ ■ I T A T ■ C H A P
B L O N D E B O M B S H E L L
■ A I R E ■ ■ A O R T A
B L U N D E R B U S S ■ B A Y
I O T A ■ C I A L I S ■ A R E
T W A S ■ T A R T L Y ■ L S D
```

27 ■ The Lost Ages

```
D U H ■ S A M E D A Y ■ S M A
I N A ■ O N E V O T E ■ N A N
T O T ■ N O T E P A S S I N G
■ M E S S I N A B O T T L E
S H A G ■ E S E ■ R I C E R
A O K A Y ■ R M S ■ P H Y S
T H E D A M I S D O N E ■ ■
S O R ■ Y E T ■ V I A ■ U K E
■ ■ G A R B D I S P O S A L
A P A R ■ C E O ■ A S H E S
T I T U S ■ ■ I A N ■ T E L E
E X T E N D E D C O V E R ■
M I L L I O N A I R E ■ O H M
P E E ■ T H I R D S T ■ U M P
O S E ■ S A D E Y E S ■ T M S
```

28 ■ Monkey Business

```
A G R O ■ F A S T ■ I Z A A K
H E E P ■ R O A R ■ M E R L E
O N B A L A N C E ■ B E G O T
Y O U R E Y E S A R E S H U T
■ A T T N ■ ■ D O C ■ ■ ■
■ ■ S A A B ■ T I P T O E
A L F A ■ B L A H ■ L E A R N
M Y L I P S A R E S E A L E D
P R A D A ■ I D L E ■ T K O S
S E W A G E ■ S L A P ■ ■ ■
■ ■ E R E ■ ■ I S N O
H I S E A R S C A N T H E A R
A S I A N ■ S A F E H O U S E
W O R S T ■ A P E S ■ P R E P
K N E E S ■ Y O W S ■ S O S O
```

29 ■ Doughnuts, Anyone?

S	C	A	M	P			P	C	B			M	A	M	B	O
S	E	L	M	A			H	U	R			A	T	A	R	I
G	O	O	D	C	H	O	L	E	S	T	E	R	O	L		
T	S	E	L	I	O	T			A	C	T	R	E	S	S	
				F	R	O	N	T	I	E	R					
		G	O	I	N	G	W	H	O	L	E	H	O	G		
C	H	I	N	S			S	T	E	N			E	A	U	
R	E	V	A	M	P				S	I	T	A	R	S		
O	S	E			U	T	E	S			M	A	R	S	H	
W	A	R	H	O	L	E	X	H	I	B	I	T				
			I	D	L	E	T	I	M	E						
A	L	A	D	D	I	N			V	A	C	C	I	N	E	
H	O	L	E	I	N	T	H	E	M	I	D	D	L	E		
A	L	O	R	S			S	I	R			L	I	B	E	L
B	L	U	S	H			Y	E	S			E	V	E	R	Y

30 ■ Picnic Fare

L	I	L			R	T	E			H	O	T	D	O	G	S
I	C	E	B	E	E	R			O	P	H	E	L	I	A	
C	A	R	O	U	S	E			H	E	A	V	I	N	G	
K	N	O	W	S	H	I	S	O	N	I	O	N	S			
S	T	Y	L	E			O	H	S							
				S	A	N	Y	O			A	A	R	O	N	
A	G	E	S			S	E	A			A	L	L	U	R	E
R	E	L	I	S	H	E	S	T	H	E	I	D	E	A		
I	N	A	L	I	E			A	U	S			T	E	S	T
P	A	N	T	S			T	U	T	O	R					
				S	E	C					A	O	R	T	A	
		C	U	T	S	T	H	E	M	U	S	T	A	R	D	
A	U	R	O	R	A	E			I	N	C	I	S	O	R	
D	E	G	R	A	D	E			R	E	A	C	T	T	O	
D	R	E	S	S	E	D			E	S	L			A	S	P

31 ■ The Fat Lady Sings

K	I	D	S			G	E	L			R	U	M	P	U	S
A	M	O	K			A	M	I			E	N	R	A	G	E
L	O	W	E			P	I	L	O	T	L	I	G	H	T	
		U	N	I	T			A	N	I			S	E	S	S
S	T	A	N	D	U	P	C	O	M	I	C					
C	A	T			S	H	Y			R	E	S	A	L	E	S
A	H	H			U	L	A				A	N	I	C	E	
G	E	E			T	H	E	R	O	C	K			N	O	T
G	R	E	B	E			M	N	O					E	S	T
S	E	L	E	C	T	S			C	D	S			D	Y	E
			C	H	A	R	L	E	Y	H	O	R	S	E		
E	L	S	A			W	I	I			S	P	I	T		
L	I	Q	U	I	D	S	O	A	P			E	V	E	L	
K	A	I	S	E	R			N	B	A			R	E	M	I
O	R	N	E	R	Y			S	E	M			A	S	S	T

32 ■ A River Runs Through It

M	O	D	E	M			D	A	S			C	L	O	A	K
E	N	A	M	I			I	M	P			R	O	N	C	O
A	S	N	E	R			C	O	Y			U	S	E	T	O
D	E	G	R	A	D	E					S	E	E	F	I	T
S	T	S			M	E	D	U	S	A			T	O	V	E
			A	I	M			N	T	H			O	R	A	N
M	D	C	C	I			H	E	L	M			A	T	A	
G	I	R	T	H			B	O	W			A	L	L	E	Y
A	L	Y			I	G	O	R			S	C	A	L	D	
T	I	A	S			E	N	S			O	K	D			
I	T	S	O			T	E	E	N	I	E			S	P	A
N	A	D	I	R	S				U	N	N	O	T	E	D	
E	N	U	R	E			M	A	T			Z	O	R	R	O
A	T	S	E	A			O	R	S			I	P	A	S	S
U	S	T	E	D			B	T	O			E	S	T	E	E

33 ■ *You're a Gem*

```
J A D E   I M H O   P E A R L
A M O S   T A I L   O R S E A
C O M P   I R M A   L O P E Z
I R E N E S   O F M E   U L U
N O S   A N E M I A   A R I L
T U T T U T S     Y E M E N I
H S I A   T O O N I E
    C O R N E R S T O N E
    I G U E S S     D A R C
G E T S T O   I N A S T I R
A L O T   V I D E O S   I V Y
R T E   I A T E   T E N N I S
N O C A N   C L I I   I G E T
E R A S E   H T T P   C U R A
T O P A Z   Y A Y S   O P A L
```

34 ■ *Hollywood North*

```
C A S A B A   P E A L   I C I
I T A L I C   R O L E   H O N
D A V I D C R O N E N B E R G
    E A S E U P   D R A N O
B E T   P E S T O   O R E O
R A I L A T   A W K W A R D
A R M E D   S O C I O
  L E S L I E N I E L S E N
    I N S E T   A P N E A
A C R O B A T   A S Y L U M
S H A H   N O T A S   I F I
H A S O N   T W I L L S
M I C H A E L O N D A A T J E
A S A   T R A P   E N D E A R
N E L   O A T S   S A Y D I E
```

35 ■ *Animal Husbandry*

```
O B O E   M A F I A S   U M S
P E A T   A T O N C E   N A T
T A K E A G A N D E R   B R R
S K Y   W I L D     D E K E
    J A C K U P P R I C E S
O H B O Y     L I E N O R S
Z O O T   C Y N I C I S M
S O B   D R O N E O N   I T T
  S L E E K E S T   O N Z E
O N L E A S E   M O G U L
S T E E R C L E A R O F
T E D S     P U T T   E M O
E S D   P A S S T H E B U C K
R T E   E L T O R O   A R C O
S S R   C A R M E N   Y O L K
```

36 ■ *Twain on Women*

```
I C A N T   C A N A D I A N
M A N I A   O H I D U N N O
A L D E R S   H A N D E D T O
G I R L S A R E S O   E O N
I C E S   I O N   B A N N S
N O T   O D E   P R E T T Y
E S T A B   P I E R S
  I T I S A R E L I E F
    T W E R E   N A O M I
N O W A N D   E K G   L O S
G E T O N   G E E   A D D R
R U T   T H E N T O S E E A
A R A P A H O E   T O O D L E
S A V O R E R S   O R I E L
P L A I N O N E   H E N R I
```

37 ■ Trading Places

```
R O U T S ■ E C C L ■ C F C S
A P N E A ■ M A R I ■ A L O W
I T S A T ■ I R A Q ■ R O O F
D I A R Y P R O D U C T S ■ ■
E M I G R E ■ ■ L O U I S I I
D A D A ■ P A P E R T R I A L
■ ■ ■ S C U B A ■ ■ L E N T E
G P S ■ A P A R A D E ■ G E S
T A L O N ■ ■ T O U R S ■ ■ ■
B R I A N C H I L D ■ H O M O
R E D R O S E ■ ■ E L O P E R
■ A S T H I N A S A R I A L ■
I C B M ■ A F I G ■ M E A D E
R U L E ■ R E N O ■ A U T O S
K E E N ■ P R O G ■ S P E W S
```

38 ■ Page Layout

```
M A O ■ R I F L E S ■ O R C A
A N S ■ O G R I S H ■ F I L E
R A T ■ T O O K A H E A D E R
G E R I ■ T Z U S ■ A S I A ■
I M I T A T E D ■ Y V O N N E
N I C E T A N ■ B E E R G U T
S C H M O ■ D N A ■ T S P S ■
■ ■ ■ B O D Y A R T ■ ■ ■ ■ ■
P A R E ■ M A E ■ W A H O O ■
O P I A T E S ■ W E A R O F F
L E S S O N ■ L A U S A N N E
■ S E E R ■ S I N G ■ B E O R
P U S S Y F O O T E R ■ S U R
S I T U ■ M A N A N A ■ T S O
T T O P ■ S P A D E D ■ Y E R
```

39 ■ [sigh]

```
B A D O F F ■ C A L L S T O
A S R A R E ■ C H E A T E R
W H A T A D R E A M B O A T
L O M ■ G O A D ■ ■ C P R ■
S E A B I R D ■ A R O U S E D
■ A L A S T I S A P I T Y ■
P U S H E S ■ I M A T ■ N A E
E T C S ■ ■ H T S ■ S T I R
P A R ■ T F A L ■ S P O O L S
T H A T S A R E L I E F ■ ■
O N T H E Q T ■ A D R A T E S
■ C R T ■ A G E S ■ W E S
T H I S I S S O B O R I N G
S E C E D E S ■ E N D S I T
P R E S A L T ■ T A S T E S
```

40 ■ Don't Bother Me

```
S E C ■ O H A R A ■ P A N G
U N O S ■ S Y S O P ■ R O I L
K A R L ■ S M I L E ■ O R C A
I M N O T I N T E R E S T E D
Y O W ■ H E S ■ ■ D I A N E
A R A C E ■ T H I S T L E S
K E L P ■ P A R A D E ■ ■
I D L I K E T O H E L P B U T
■ ■ ■ I R A I S E ■ E A C H
G L A D D E N S ■ S I D L E
R O B E D ■ ■ S A N ■ B U R
I T S N O T M Y P R O B L E M
L I E S ■ E I E I O ■ O O L A
S O N E ■ A C T T O ■ N O E L
E N T R ■ S E I S M ■ D T S
```

41 ■ Closet Disorganizer

```
A T D A W N   O S S A   L I P
S H A N I A   S E A N   A N N
M O D E L T S H I R T   T A E
A S O   L I E   Z T I L E S
D E E D   O T T E R   O F N O
  D O W N U N D E R W E A R
    C H A P S   U S E R S
A C S   A L S   F M S   S L O
T U N I C   P R I S M
T R I C K K N E E S O C K
N E V E   L A C E R   S L I D
  A E R I E S   S E M   U N O
I L L   F I S H T A N K T O P
I L E   I N E S   D O O Z I E
I S R   T E R N   S P R Y L Y
```

42 ■ Don't Make Me Laugh

```
M A Y B E   C O P   F R A M E
O R O U T   A L L   L I N E D
J O H N C A N D Y   O C T A D
O N O S   I A M   P O K I L Y
      E L L A   A R M
T O A D S   S I N S   E S A S
A G H A S T   D I S T R U S T
I R O N E R S   T E A C A K E
G E R A N I U M   S T E V I E
A S A Y   F E E S   T R E N D
    K A L   A W A Y
D E A R M E   T A R   F E L T
A N J O U   J I M C A R R E Y
S T A Y S   L E I   N O I S E
H O R D E   O R S   T E N S E
```

43 ■ Tangled Fishing Lines

```
M A N I A C   R I B   I O W E
F R A N C A   A T M   S N A X
O N S Q U I D R O W   A T I C
R O T   M A I   L A H T I
    P R A W N B R O K E R S
  T E E I N G   Y E P   B E E
  O P E L   R N A   H I S S
  W I L L D O C O D J O B S
W E T S   I R A   E L L E
E R O   E S C   S H A D E S
N A M E T H A T T U N A
T B I R D   E N G   H E P
B O Z O   M U S S E L C A R S
A V E S   O F T   S A I D I T
D E D E   T O Y   T O R I E S
```

44 ■ Much of Canada

```
C H A T T E D   I N H A S T E
D E G R A D E   Q U A K I N G
T R O O P E R   S E V E N T O
    P E N N E   V E Y
S O L I D   C L A N   D E F
S P A C E R A C E   O N E P M
H E Y   C O M E T S   A V I S
  R O C K S A N D T R E E S
T A V I   E N T I R E   L O M
S T E V E   D R E S S C O D E
K E R   V R A I   A S P E N
    L E O   C H A M P
K O L A N U T   O P P O S E D
G R A N I T E   S A L T I E R
B R I E F E D   T R E S T L E
```

45 ■ Inflated Language

```
O S A Y   G R R   S L O A N E
O H N O   L E E   P A S S A S
D E A R J O H N   A R A B I C
L I K E A B A D N I C K E L
E L I   N E B   I N H A S T E
S A N T E   S A X     T I D
    O D D   P E T S H O P S
  W O O D E N D I M E S
O M E L E T T E   M I X
H E T     H A T   L A P O F
M A S C A R A   O N E   A N A
  T U R N O N A Q U A R T E R
A P I A N O   G U T T U R A L
N I T W I T   R E S   B I L E
Y E S S E S   O S O   E A S Y
```

46 ■ Name That Beer

```
P I S T O L S   A B O L I S H
A N T O N I O   R E L A P S E
C H A R I O T   C L A M O R S
M O L S O N   C A I N E
A M A I N   W A D E D   P L O
N E G   S T O R E S   T O I L
    C A R R E     S H O N E
  C A R L I N G O K E E F E
B O R A T     I M E A N
A R A B   D I V A N S   A T M
Y E R   K A R E N   C U T I E
    S E N O R   L A B A T T
R E A L I G N   R I P O S T E
E N T I T L E   S K E L T E R
F E A T H E R   T E S T E R S
```

47 ■ Let's Get Atter!

```
I N A   P S T S   A S T A R T
C O T   H O W E   P E E L E R
E N T R Y F E E   I N S I D E
S P L A T T E R B A T T E R
I R E N E S     I N A S N I T
N O E L   H E A D O N   A V E
    A S O U R     O F T E N
  H A T T E R C H A T T E R
G O N E R     E R I E S
E M G   E V A D E R   M A S T
T E E H E E D     P O I N T E
  P L A T T E R C L A T T E R
R A I L A T   S L A T H E R S
I G N O R E   V I N E   E E E
B E A S T S   P I E S   D O R
```

48 ■ Going on a French Diet

```
H O P S   S T O I C   C A L F
E L L A   O H A R A   E S A U
R E A M   D E T A T   S K I N
B O N E H O M M E   S T A C K
A L E   O I S E   S I S
L E T B E   A L L R I G H T
    O R I L L I A   B R A D
M E A N S T O   C Y B O R G S
E L S E   W O R K S O N
G L A C I A T E   W E E D S
    H R S   C O S I   T A L
A L G A E   T E R R E B O N E
L O O N   M A D A T   E I N E
A V E C   G R E T A   S L O P
S E R E   B O D E S   T E N S
```

49 ■ *The Opposite Effect*

50 ■ *Sing Me a Song*

MORE
O Canada Crosswords!

    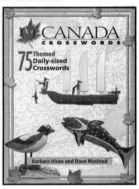

With their distinctive folk-art covers and uniquely Canadian content, the *O Canada Crosswords* books have garnered a devoted fan base of crossword aficionados from coast to coast. Spellings are Canadian too, and many words are derived from our history, geography and pop culture.

O Canada Crosswords, Book 1, 115 Great Canadian Crosswords • 8½ x 11, 136 pp, pb
978-1-894404-02-0 • $14.95

O Canada Crosswords, Book 2, 50 Giant Weekend-size Crosswords • 8½ x 11, 120 pp, pb
978-1-894404-04-4 • $14.95

O Canada Crosswords, Book 3, 50 More Giant Weekend Crosswords • 8½ x 11, 120 pp, pb
978-1-894404-11-2 • $14.95

O Canada Crosswords, Book 4, 50 Incredible Giant Weekend Crosswords • 8½ x 11, 120 pp, pb
978-1-894404-18-1 • $14.95

O Canada Crosswords, Book 5, 50 Fantastic Giant Weekend Crosswords • 8½ x 11, 120 pp, pb
978-1-894404-20-4 • $14.95

O Canada Crosswords, Book 6, 50 Great Weekend-size Crosswords • 8½ x 11, 120 pp, pb
978-0-88971-206-5 • $14.95

O Canada Crosswords, Book 7, 50 Wonderful Weekend-size Crosswords • 8½ x 11, 120 pp, pb
978-0-88971-218-8 • $14.95

O Canada Crosswords Book 8, 75 Themed Daily-sized Crosswords • 8½ x 11, 176 pp, pb
978-0-88971-217-1 • $12.95

O Canada Crosswords, Book 9, 75 Themed Daily-sized Crosswords • 8½ x 11, 115 pp, pb
978-0-88971-225-6 • $12.95